THE BIBLE

NEW TESTAMENT

THE BIBLE

NEW TESTAMENT

ILLUSTRATED SELECTIONS

Above: Detail from THE ASSUMPTION *by Bernadino Bergognone*

Opposite: ADORATION OF THE MAGI, *German School*

A John Macrae Book
HENRY HOLT AND COMPANY
NEW YORK

Henry Holt and Company, Inc.
Publishers since 1866
115 West 18th Street
New York, New York 10011

Henry Holt® is a registered trademark of Henry Holt and Company, Inc.

First published in the United States in 1995 by
Henry Holt and Company, Inc.
Originally published in Great Britain in 1995 by Ebury Press, an imprint of the Random House Group.

Library of Congress Catalog Card Number is available upon request.

ISBN 0-8050-4125-7

Henry Holt books are available for special promotions and premiums. For details contact: Director, Special markets.

First American Edition – 1995

Selected and edited by Joanne Cracknell
Designed by David Fordham
Picture research by Gabrielle Allen

Printed in Singapore

1 3 5 7 9 10 8 6 4 2

THE BIBLE

NEW TESTAMENT

Contents

Preface

It is hoped that the present selection will provide a fresh insight into the heart of the New Testament, whilst retaining the beauty and dignity of the Authorized Version.

In making the necessary abridgement, the balance of the original has been maintained, so that about half the text consists of extracts from the four Gospels. In order to produce a coherent narrative whilst representing each Gospel writer fairly, these extracts have been re-arranged into roughly chronological order.

It must be emphasized that, although actual contradictions have been avoided, this is in no sense an attempt to produce a single harmonious story of the life of Christ. The individual perspective of the Fourth Gospel, if nothing else, would make such an attempt impossible.

Nevertheless, it is hoped that this selection, in focusing on the fullest, best-known and most vivid Gospel stories, will shed new light on the person of Jesus Christ and on the lives and teachings of his followers.

Acknowledgements

Bayerische Staatsgemäldesammlungen, Munich 48
Bridgeman Art Library 3 (Brera Gallery, Milan), 8 (Alte Pinakathek, Munich), 15 (Galleria dell'Accademia, Venice), 16 (Prado, Madrid), 22 (Galleria dell'Accademia, Venice), 23 (Galleria degli Uffizi, Florence), 25 (Prado, Madrid), 26 (Jean Paul Getty Museum, Malibu), 37 (Pushkin Museum, Moscow), 55 (Guildhall Art Gallery, Corporation of London), 58 (Prado, Madrid, 60 (Private Collection), 67 (Museo Correr, Venice), 72 (Courtauld Institute Galleries, University of London), 78 (Kunsthistorisches Museum, Vienna), 81 (Hotel Dieu, Beaune), 86 (Hermitage, St Petersburg), 95 (Prado, Madrid), 99 (Museo dell'Opera del Duomo, Siena), 101 (Scrovegni Chapel, Padua), 104 (Christie's, London), 106 (Museo Figline, Valdarno), 108 (Museo dell'Opera del Duomo, Siena), 109 (Prado, Madrid), 111 (Museodell'Opera del Duomo, Siena), 117 (Capilla Real,

Granada), 118 (Museo di San Marco dell'Angelico, Florence), 120 (Scrovegni Chapel, Padua), 124 (Prado, Madrid), 126 (Prado, Madrid), 127 (Church of St Agostino, Siena), 129 (Galleria dell'Accademia, Florence), 130 (Galleria Degli Uffizi, Florence), 132 (Museo di San Marco dell'Angelico, Florence), 138 (Victoria and Albert Museum, London), 139 (Belvoir Castle, Leicestershire), 140 (Santa Maria del Carmine, Florence), 148 (Victoria and Albert Museum, London), 150 (Vatican, Rome), 153 (Museum of Fine Arts, Budapest), 158 (Rafael Valls Gallery, London), 165 (Hermitage, St Petersburg), 167 (Cecil Higgins Art Gallery, Bedford), 176 (Prado, Madrid), 179 (Alan Jacobs Gallery, London), 192/193 (Lutherhalle, Wittenberg), 197 (Scuola di San Rocco, Venice), 200 (Villa Loschi, Vicenza), 202 (Academia de San Fernando, Madrid), 205 (Galleria dell'Accademia, Venice), 209 (Galleria dell'Accademia, Venice), 212 (Galleria dell'Accademia, Florence), 225 (Christie's, London), 235 (Kunsthistorisches Museum, Vienna), 239 (Villa Loschi, Vicenza), 241 (Vatican, Rome), 242 (Brera Gallery, Milan), 244 (Biblioteca Marciana, Venice), 247 (Prado, Madrid), 250 (Wallace Collection, London), 255 (Memling Museum, Bruges), 257 (Scrovegni Chapel, Padua), 263 (Prado, Madrid), 267 (Wallraf-Richartz Museum , Cologne), 271 (Prado, Madrid)

Fundación Colección Thyssen-Bornemisza, Madrid 28, 50

Giraudon/Bridgeman Art Library 2 (Musée des Beaux-Arts, Lille), 12 (Musée des Beaux-Arts, Nantes), 30 (Musée des Beaux-Arts, Nantes), 33 (Louvre, Paris), 40 (Musée des Beaux-Arts, Le Havre), 47 (Musée des Beaux-Arts, Marseilles), 93 (Louvre, Paris), 135 (Musée des Beaux-Arts, Nantes), 145 (Musée des Beaux-Arts, Nantes), 163 (Musée des Beaux-Arts, Nantes), 182 (Cathedral of St Bravo, Ghent), 189 (Louvre, Paris), 208 (Louvre, Paris), 215 (Louvre, Paris), 227 (Cathedral of St Bravo, Ghent)

Metropolitan Museum of Art, New York 31, 59

National Gallery, London 21, 75

National Gallery of Scotland, Edinburgh 230

Neues Palais, Potsdam 136

The Royal Collection © Her Majesty Queen Elizabeth II 154

Scala 19 (St Maria Novella, Florence), 43 (Galleria dell'Accademia, Venice), 44 (Sistine Chapel, Vatican, Rome), 62 (Museo dell'Opera Metropolitana, Siena), 88 (Galleria dell'Accademia, Venice), 143 (Scrovegni Chapel, Padua), 157 (St Maria del Popolo, Rome), 171 (Pinacoteca Nazionale, Siena), 181 (Pinacoteca Nazionale, Siena), 220 (Duomo, Orvieto), 252 (Museo di St Marco, Florence), 260 (Gabinetto dei Disegni e dell Stampe, Florence)

Wallace Collection, London 269

Chapter & Verses FROM THE GOSPELS

ACCORDING TO
ST. MATTHEW
ST. MARK
ST. LUKE
& ST. JOHN

THE ANNUNCIATION *by Rogier van der Weyden*

The Gospels According to Matthew, Mark, Luke and John

The word made flesh (John) • ZACHARIAS AND ELISABETH (Luke) • THE ANGEL APPEARS TO MARY (Luke) • THE BIRTH OF JOHN THE BAPTIST (Luke) • THE BIRTH OF CHRIST (Luke) • THE VISIT OF THE WISE MEN (Matthew) • THE BOY JESUS IN THE TEMPLE (Luke) • THE BAPTISM OF JESUS (Matthew) • JESUS IS TEMPTED IN THE WILDERNESS (Matthew) • THE CALLING OF THE FIRST DISCIPLES (Mark) • THE MARRIAGE AT CANA (John) • JESUS AND NICODEMUS (John) • JESUS AND THE WOMAN OF SAMARIA (John) • A HEALING AT CAPERNAUM (Mark) • THE CALLING OF MATTHEW (Matthew) • LORD OF THE SABBATH (Mark) • THE APPOINTMENT OF THE TWELVE APOSTLES (Luke) • THE SERMON ON THE MOUNT (Matthew) • "LOVE YOUR ENEMIES" (Matthew) • TREASURES IN HEAVEN (Matthew) • THE CENTURION'S SERVANT (Luke) • JESUS RAISES A WIDOW'S SON (Luke) • THE PARABLE OF THE SOWER (Mark) • PARABLES OF THE KINGDOM (I) (Matthew) • PARABLES OF THE KINGDOM (II) (Mark) • JESUS STILLS THE STORM (Mark) • THE GADARENE SWINE (Mark) • JAIRUS'S DAUGHTER (Mark) • JESUS REJECTED AT NAZARETH (Luke) • JOHN THE BAPTIST BEHEADED (Mark) • THE FEEDING OF THE FIVE THOUSAND (John) • JESUS WALKS ON WATER (Matthew) • THE BREAD OF LIFE (John) • THE FAITH OF THE WOMAN OF CANAAN (Matthew) • PETER'S CONFESSION (Luke) • THE TRANSFIGURATION (Matthew) • JESUS HEALS A BOY WITH A DUMB SPIRIT (Mark) • THE GREATEST IN THE KINGDOM OF HEAVEN (Matthew) • THE PARABLE OF THE UNMERCIFUL SERVANT (Matthew) • JESUS TEACHES IN THE

TEMPLE AT THE FEAST OF THE TABERNACLES (John) • THE WOMAN TAKEN IN ADULTERY (John) • THE LIGHT OF THE WORLD (John) • JESUS HEALS A MAN BLIND FROM BIRTH (John) • THE GOOD SHEPHERD (John) • THE PARABLE OF THE GOOD SAMARITAN (Luke) • MARTHA AND MARY (Luke) • THE LORD'S PRAYER (Luke) • THE STRAIT GATE (Luke) • THE PARABLE OF THE GREAT BANQUET (Luke) • THE PARABLES OF THE LOST SHEEP AND THE LOST COIN (Luke) • THE PARABLE OF THE PRODIGAL SON (Luke) • THE PARABLE OF THE RICH MAN AND LAZARUS (Luke) • THE PARABLE OF THE PHARISEE AND THE PUBLICAN (Luke) • JESUS BLESSES LITTLE CHILDREN (Mark) • THE RICH YOUNG MAN (Mark) • THE PARABLE OF THE LABOURERS IN THE VINEYARD (Matthew) • BLIND BARTIMAEUS (Mark) • ZACCHEAEUS (Luke) • THE RAISING OF LAZARUS (John) • JESUS ANOINTED AT BETHANY (John) • THE TRIUMPHAL ENTRY (Luke) • THE CLEANSING OF THE TEMPLE (Matthew) • THE AUTHORITY OF JESUS QUESTIONED (Luke) • THE GREATEST COMMANDMENT (Mark) • THE WIDOW'S MITES (Mark) • SIGNS OF THE END OF THE WORLD (Matthew) • THE PARABLE OF THE TEN VIRGINS (Matthew) • THE PARABLE OF THE TALENTS (Matthew) • THE SHEEP AND THE GOATS (Matthew) • JUDAS AGREES TO BETRAY JESUS (Luke) • THE LAST SUPPER (Luke) • JESUS WASHES HIS DISCIPLES' FEET (John) • A NEW COMMANDMENT (John) • THE WAY, THE TRUTH AND THE LIFE (John) • THE TRUE VINE (John) • "ASK, AND YE SHALL RECIEVE" (John) • GETHSEMANE (Matthew) • JESUS BEFORE CAIAPHAS (Matthew) • JUDAS HANGS HIMSELF (Matthew) • JESUS BEFORE PILATE (John) • THE CRUCIFIXION (Luke) • JESUS LAID IN THE TOMB (Matthew) • THE RESURRECTION (John) • THE WALK TO EMMAUS (Luke) • DOUBTING THOMAS (John) • PETER'S REINSTATEMENT (John) • THE GREAT COMMISSION (Matthew) •

The Word Made Flesh

John 1:1-14

John 1

IN THE BEGINNING WAS THE WORD, AND THE WORD was with God, and the Word was God. [2]The same was in the beginning with God.

[3]All things were made by him; and without him was not any thing made that was made. [4]In him was life; and the life was the light of men. [5]And the light shineth in darkness; and the darkness comprehended it not.

John the Baptist in the Wilderness *by Guido Reni*

John 1

[6]There was a man sent from God; whose name was John. [7]The same came for a witness, to bear witness of the Light, that all men through him might believe. [8]He was not that Light, but was sent to bear witness of that Light. [9]That was the true Light, which lighteth every man that cometh into the world.

[10]He was in the world, and the world was made by him, and the world knew him not. [11]He came unto his own, and his own received him not. [12]But as many as received him, to them gave he power to become the sons of God, even to them that believe on his name: [13]which were born, not of blood, nor of the will of the flesh, nor of the will of man, but of God.

[14]And the Word was made flesh, and dwelt among us, (and we beheld his glory, the glory as of the only begotten of the Father), full of grace and truth.

Zacharias and Elisabeth

Luke 1:5-25

Luke 1

THERE WAS IN THE DAYS OF HEROD, THE KING OF Judaea, a certain priest named Zacharias, of the course of Abia: and his wife was of the daughters of Aaron, and her name was Elisabeth. [6]And they were both righteous before God, walking in all the commandments and ordinances of the Lord blameless. [7]And they had no child, because that Elisabeth was barren, and they both were now well stricken in years.

[8]And it came to pass, that while he executed the priest's office before God in the order of his course, [9]according to the custom of the priest's office, his lot was to burn incense when he went into the temple of the Lord. [10]And the whole multitude of the people were praying without at the time of incense.

[11]And there appeared unto him an angel of the Lord standing on the right side of the altar of incense. [12]And when Zacharias saw him, he was troubled, and fear fell

upon him. [13]But the angel said unto him, "Fear not, Zacharias: for thy prayer is heard; and thy wife Elisabeth shall bear thee a son, and thou shalt call his name John. [14]And thou shalt have joy and gladness; and many shall rejoice at his birth. [15]For he shall be great in the sight of the Lord, and shall drink neither wine nor strong drink; and he shall be filled with the Holy Ghost, even from his mother's womb. [16]And many of the children of Israel shall he turn to the Lord their God. [17]And he shall go before him in the spirit and power of Elias, to turn the hearts of the fathers to the children, and the disobedient to the wisdom of the just; to make ready a people prepared for the Lord."

[18]And Zacharias said unto the angel, "Whereby shall I know this? For I am an old man and my wife well stricken in years."

[19]And the angel answering said unto him, "I am Gabriel, that stand in the presence of God; and am sent to speak unto thee, and to shew thee these glad tidings. [20]And, behold, thou shalt be dumb, and not able to speak, until the day that these things shall be performed, because thou believest not my words, which shall be fulfilled in their season."

[21]And the people waited for Zacharias, and marvelled that he tarried so long in the temple. [22]And when he came out, he could not speak unto them: and they perceived that he had seen a vision in the temple: for he beckoned unto them, and remained speechless.

[23]And it came to pass, that, as soon as the days of his ministration were accomplished, he departed to his own house. [24]And after those days his wife Elisabeth conceived, and hid herself five months, saying, [25]"Thus hath the Lord dealt with me in the days wherein he looked on me, to take away my reproach among men."

The Archangel Gabriel *by Jacopo da Montagnana*

The Angel Appears to Mary

Luke 1:26-56

Luke 1

AND IN THE SIXTH MONTH THE ANGEL GABRIEL was sent from God unto a city of Galilee, named Nazareth, [27]to a virgin espoused to a man whose name was Joseph, of the house of David; and the virgin's name was Mary. [28]And the angel came in unto her, and said, "Hail, thou that art highly favoured, the Lord is with thee: blessed art thou among women."

[29]And when she saw him, she was troubled at his saying, and cast in her mind what manner of salutation this should be. [30]And the angel said unto her, "Fear not, Mary: for thou hast found favour with God. [31]And, behold, thou shalt conceive in thy womb, and bring forth a son, and shalt call his name JESUS. [32]He shall be great, and shall be called the Son of the Highest: and the Lord God shall give unto him the throne of his father David: [33]and he shall

The Annunciation *by Fra Angelico*

reign over the house of Jacob for ever; and of his kingdom there shall be no end."

[34]Then said Mary unto the angel, "How shall this be, seeing I know not a man?"

[35]And the angel answered and said unto her, "The Holy Ghost shall come upon thee, and the power of the Highest shall overshadow thee: therefore also that holy thing which shall be born of thee shall be called the Son of God. [36]And, behold, thy cousin Elisabeth, she hath also conceived a son in her old age: and this is the sixth month with her, who was called barren. [37]For with God nothing shall be impossible."

[38]And Mary said, "Behold the handmaid of the Lord; be it unto me according to thy word." And the angel departed from her.

[39]And Mary arose in those days, and went into the hill country with haste, into a city of Juda; [40]and entered into the house of Zacharias, and saluted Elisabeth. [41]And it came to pass, that, when Elisabeth heard the salutation of Mary, the babe leaped in her womb; and Elisabeth was filled with the Holy Ghost: [42]and she spake out with a loud voice, and said, "Blessed art thou among women, and blessed is the fruit of thy womb.

[43]And whence is this to me, that the mother of my Lord should come to me? [44]For, lo, as soon as the voice of thy salutation sounded in mine ears, the babe leaped in my womb for joy. [45]And blessed is she that believed: for there shall be a performance of those things which were told her from the Lord."

[46]And Mary said,
"My soul doth magnify the Lord,
[47]And my spirit hath rejoiced in God my Saviour.
[48]For he hath regarded
The low estate of his handmaiden:
For, behold, from henceforth
All generations shall call me blessed.
[49]For he that is mighty hath done to me great things;
And holy is his name.
[50]And his mercy is on them that fear him
From generation to generation.
[51]He hath shewed strength with his arm;

Luke 1

He hath scattered the proud in the imagination of their hearts.
[52]He hath put down the mighty from their seats,
And exalted them of low degree.
[53]He hath filled the hungry with good things;
And the rich he hath sent empty away.
[54]He hath holpen his servant Israel,
In remembrance of his mercy;
[55]As he spake to our fathers,
To Abraham, and to his seed for ever."

[56]And Mary abode with her about three months, and returned to her own house.

The Birth of John the Baptist

Luke 1:57-80

Luke 1

Now Elisabeth's full time came that she should be delivered; and she brought forth a son. [58]And her neighbours and her cousins heard how the Lord had shewed great mercy upon her; and they rejoiced with her.

[59]And it came to pass, that on the eighth day they came to circumcise the child; and they called him Zacharias, after the name of his father. [60]And his mother answered and said, "Not so; but he shall be called John."

[61]And they said unto her, "There is none of thy kindred that is called by this name."

[62]And they made signs to his father, how he would have him called. [63]And he asked for a writing table, and wrote, saying, "His name is John." And they marvelled all.

[64]And his mouth was opened immediately, and his tongue loosed, and he spake, and praised God. [65]And fear came on all that dwelt round about them: and all these sayings were noised abroad throughout all the hill country of Judaea. [66]And all they that heard them laid them up in their hearts, saying, "What manner of child shall this be!" And the hand of the Lord was with him.

Luke 1

THE BIRTH OF JOHN THE BAPTIST *by Domenico Ghirlandaio*

[67]And his father Zacharias was filled with the Holy Ghost, and prophesied, saying,

Luke 1

[68]"Blessed be the Lord God of Israel;
For he hath visited and redeemed his people,
[69]And hath raised up an horn of salvation for us
In the house of his servant David;
[70]As he spake by the mouth of his holy prophets,
Which have been since the world began:
[71]That we should be saved from our enemies,
And from the hand of all that hate us,
[72]To perform the mercy promised to our fathers,
And to remember his holy covenant;
[73]The oath which he sware to our father Abraham,
[74]That he would grant unto us,

Luke 1

That we being delivered out of the hand of our enemies
Might serve him without fear,
75 In holiness and righteousness before him,
All the days of our life.
76 And thou, child, shalt be called the prophet of the Highest:
For thou shalt go before the face of the Lord to prepare his ways;
77 To give knowledge of salvation unto his people
By the remission of their sins,
78 Through the tender mercy of our God;
Whereby the dayspring from on high hath visited us,
79 To give light to them that sit in darkness
And in the shadow of death,
To guide our feet into the way of peace."

80 And the child grew, and waxed strong in spirit, and was in the deserts till the day of his shewing unto Israel.

The Birth of Christ

Luke 2:1-38

Luke 2

AND IT CAME TO PASS IN THOSE DAYS, THAT THERE went out a decree from Caesar Augustus, that all the world should be taxed. 2 (And this taxing was first made when Cyrenius was governor of Syria.) 3 And all went to be taxed, every one into his own city.

4 And Joseph also went up from Galilee, out of the city of Nazareth, into Judaea, unto the city of David, which is called Bethlehem; (because he was of the house and lineage of David:) 5 to be taxed with Mary his espoused wife, being great with child. 6 And so it was, that, while they were there, the days were accomplished that she should be delivered. 7 And she brought forth her firstborn son, and wrapped him in swaddling clothes, and laid him in a manger; because there was no room for them in the inn.

8 And there were in the same country shepherds abiding in the field, keeping watch over their flock by night. 9 And,

THE VIRGIN AND CHILD *by Domenico Ghirlandaio*

Luke 2

MADONNA AND CHILD WITH JOHN THE BAPTIST *by Giovanni Bellini and Tiziano Titian*

Luke 2

lo, the angel of the Lord came upon them, and the glory of the Lord shone round about them: and they were sore afraid. [10]And the angel said unto them, "Fear not: for, behold, I bring you good tidings of great joy, which shall be to all people. [11]For unto you is born this day in the city of David a Saviour, which is Christ the Lord. [12]And this shall be a sign unto you; ye shall find the babe wrapped in swaddling clothes, lying in a manger."

[13]And suddenly there was with the angel a multitude of the heavenly host praising God, and saying, [14]"Glory to God in the highest, and on earth peace, good will toward men."

[15]And it came to pass, as the angels were gone away from them into heaven, the shepherds said one to another, "Let us now go even unto Bethlehem, and see this thing which is come to pass, which the Lord hath made known unto us."

[16]And they came with haste, and found Mary, and Joseph, and the babe lying in a manger. [17]And when they had seen it, they made known abroad the saying which was told them concerning this child. [18]And all they that heard it wondered at those things which were told them by the shepherds. [19]But Mary kept all these things and pondered

them in her heart. [20]And the shepherds returned, glorifying and praising God for all the things that they had heard and seen, as it was told unto them.

[21]And when eight days were accomplished for the circumcising of the child, his name was called JESUS, which was so named of the angel before he was conceived in the womb.

[22]And when the days of her purification according to the law of Moses were accomplished, they brought him to Jerusalem, to present him to the Lord: [23](as it is written in the law of the Lord, "Every male that openeth the womb shall be called holy to the Lord;") [24]and to offer a sacrifice according to that which is said in the law of the Lord, "A pair of turtledoves, or two young pigeons."

Adoration of the Shepherds *by Lorenzo di Credi*

Luke 2

[25]And behold, there was a man in Jerusalem, whose name was Simeon; and the same man was just and devout, waiting for the consolation of Israel: and the Holy Ghost was upon him. [26]And it was revealed unto him by the Holy Ghost, that he should not see death, before he had seen the Lord's Christ. [27]And he came by the Spirit into the temple: and when the parents brought in the child Jesus, to do for him after the custom of the law, [28]then took he him up in his arms, and blessed God, and said,

[29]"Lord, now lettest thou thy servant depart in peace,
According to thy word:
[30]For mine eyes have seen thy salvation,
[31]Which thou hast prepared before the face of all people;
[32]A light to lighten the Gentiles,
And the glory of thy people Israel."

[33]And Joseph and his mother marvelled at those things which were spoken of him. [34]And Simeon blessed them, and said unto Mary his mother, "Behold, this child is set for the fall and rising again of many in Israel; and for a sign which shall be spoken against; [35](yea, a sword shall pierce through thy own soul also,) that the thoughts of many hearts may be revealed."

[36]And there was one Anna, a prophetess, the daughter of Phanuel, of the tribe of Aser: she was of a great age, and had lived with an husband seven years from her virginity: [37]and she was a widow of about fourscore and four years, which departed not from the temple, but served God with fastings and prayers night and day. [38]And she coming in that instant gave thanks likewise unto the Lord, and spake of him to all them that looked for redemption in Jerusalem.

The Visit of the Wise Men

Matthew 2

Matthew 2

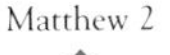

NOW WHEN JESUS WAS BORN IN BETHLEHEM OF Judaea in the days of Herod the king, behold, there came wise men from the east to Jerusalem, [2]saying, "Where is he that is born King of the Jews? For we have seen his star in the east, and are come to worship him."

[3]When Herod the king had heard these things, he was troubled, and all Jerusalem with him. [4]And when he had gathered all the chief priests and scribes of the people together, he demanded of them where Christ should be born. [5]And they said unto him, "In Bethlehem of Judaea: for thus it is written by the prophet,

> [6]"'And thou Bethlehem, in the land of Juda,
> Art not the least among the princes of Juda:
> For out of thee shall come a Governor,
> That shall rule my people Israel.'"

[7]Then Herod, when he had privily called the wise men, inquired of them diligently what time the star appeared.

Centre panel of ADORATION OF THE MAGI *by Hans Memling*

Matthew 2

ADORATION OF THE MAGI *by Andrea Mantegna*

Matthew 2

[8]And he sent them to Bethlehem and said, "Go and search diligently for the young child; and when ye have found him, bring me word again, that I may come and worship him also."

[9]When they had heard the king, they departed; and, lo, the star, which they saw in the east, went before them, till it came and stood over where the young child was. [10]When they saw the star, they rejoiced with exceeding great joy. [11]And when they were come into the house, they saw the young child with Mary his mother, and fell down, and worshipped him: and when they had opened their treasures, they presented unto him gifts: gold, and frankincense, and myrrh. [12]And being warned of God in a dream that they should not return to Herod, they departed into their own country another way.

[13]And when they were departed, behold, the angel of the Lord appeareth to Joseph in a dream, saying, "Arise, and take the young child and his mother, and flee into Egypt, and be thou there until I bring thee word: for Herod will seek the young child to destroy him."

[14]When he arose, he took the young child and his mother by night, and departed into Egypt: [15]and was there until the death of Herod: that it might be fulfilled which

Matthew 2

was spoken of the Lord by the prophet, saying, "Out of Egypt have I called my son."

[16]Then Herod, when he saw that he was mocked of the wise men, was exceeding wroth, and sent forth, and slew all the children that were in Bethlehem, and in all the coasts thereof, from two years old and under, according to the time which he had diligently inquired of the wise men. [17]Then was fulfilled that which was spoken by Jeremy the prophet, saying,

> [18]"In Rama was there a voice heard,
> Lamentation, and weeping, and great mourning,
> Rachel weeping for her children,
> And would not be comforted,
> Because they are not."

[19]But when Herod was dead, behold, an angel of the Lord appeareth in a dream to Joseph in Egypt, [20]saying, "Arise, and take the young child and his mother, and go into the land of Israel: for they are dead which sought the young child's life."

[21]And he arose, and took the young child and his mother, and came into the land of Israel. [22]But when he heard that Archelaus did reign in Judaea in the room of his father Herod, he was afraid to go thither: notwithstanding, being warned of God in a dream, he turned aside into the parts of Galilee: [23]and he came and dwelt in a city called Nazareth: that it might be fulfilled which was spoken by the prophets, "He shall be called a Nazarene."

The Boy Jesus in the Temple

Luke 2:40-52

Luke 2

And the child grew, and waxed strong in spirit, filled with wisdom: and the grace of God was upon him.

[41]Now his parents went to Jerusalem every year at the feast of the passover. [42]And when he was twelve years old, they went up to Jerusalem

Luke 2

CHRIST AMONG THE DOCTORS *by Albrecht Dürer*

Luke 2

after the custom of the feast. 43And when they had fulfilled the days, as they returned, the child Jesus tarried behind in Jerusalem; and Joseph and his mother knew not of it. 44But they, supposing him to have been in the company, went a day's journey; and they sought him among their kinsfolk and acquaintance. 45And when they found him not, they turned back again to Jerusalem, seeking him. 46And it came to pass, that after three days they found him in the temple, sitting in the midst of the doctors, both hearing them, and asking them questions. 47And all that heard him were astonished at his understanding and answers. 48And when they saw him, they were amazed: and his mother said unto him, "Son, why hast thou thus dealt with us? Behold, thy father and I have sought thee sorrowing."

49And he said unto them, "How is it that ye sought me? Wist ye not that I must be about my Father's business?" 50And they understood not the saying which he spake unto them.

51And he went down with them, and came to Nazareth, and was subject unto them: but his mother kept all these sayings in her heart. 52And Jesus increased in wisdom and stature, and in favour with God and man.

The Baptism of Jesus

Matthew 3

Matthew 3

IN THOSE DAYS CAME JOHN THE BAPTIST, PREACHING in the wilderness of Judaea, [2]and saying, "Repent ye: for the kingdom of heaven is at hand." [3]For this is he that was spoken of by the prophet Esaias, saying,

"The voice of one crying in the wilderness,
Prepare ye the way of the Lord,
Make his paths straight."

[4]And the same John had his raiment of camel's hair, and a leathern girdle about his loins; and his meat was locusts and wild honey. [5]Then went out to him Jerusalem, and all Judaea, and all the region round about Jordan, [6]and were baptized of him in Jordan, confessing their sins.

[7]But when he saw many of the Pharisees and Sadducees come to his baptism, he said unto them, "O generation of vipers, who hath warned you to flee from the wrath to come? [8]Bring forth therefore fruits meet for repentance: [9]and think not to say within yourselves, 'We have Abraham to our father': for I say unto you, that God is able of these stones to raise up children unto Abraham. [10]And now also the axe is laid unto the root of the trees: therefore every tree which bringeth not forth good fruit is hewn down, and cast into the fire.

[11]"I Indeed baptize you with water unto repentance: but he that cometh after me is mightier than I, whose shoes I am not worthy to bear: he shall baptize you with the Holy Ghost, and with fire; [12]whose fan is in his hand, and he will thoroughly purge his floor, and gather his wheat into the garner; but he will burn up the chaff with unquenchable fire."

[13]Then cometh Jesus from Galilee to Jordan unto John, to be baptized of him. [14]But John forbad him, saying, "I have need to be baptized of thee, and comest thou to me?"

[15]And Jesus answering said unto him: "Suffer it to be so now: for thus it becometh us to fulfil all righteousness." Then he suffered him.

Matthew 3

THE BAPTISM OF CHRIST *by Ottavio Vannini*

Matthew 3

[16]And Jesus, when he was baptized, went up straightway out of the water: and, lo, the heavens were opened unto him, and he saw the Spirit of God descending like a dove, and lighting upon him: [17]and lo a voice from heaven, saying, "This is my beloved Son, in whom I am well pleased."

Jesus is Tempted in the Wilderness

Matthew 4:1-11

Matthew 4

THEN WAS JESUS LED UP OF THE SPIRIT INTO THE wilderness to be tempted of the devil. [2]And when he had fasted forty days and forty nights, he was afterward an hungred. [3]And when the tempter came to him, he said, "If thou be the Son of God, command that these stones be made bread."

[4]But he answered and said, "It is written, 'Man shall not live by bread alone, but by every word that proceedeth out of the mouth of God.'"

[5]Then the devil taketh him up into the holy city, and setteth him on a pinnacle of the temple, [6]and saith unto him, "If thou be the Son of God, cast thyself down: for it is written,

"'He shall give his angels charge concerning thee:
And in their hands they shall bear thee up,
Lest at any time thou dash thy foot against a stone.'"

Christ in the Wilderness *by Moretto da Brescia*

Matthew 4

[7]Jesus said unto him, "It is written again, 'Thou shalt not tempt the Lord thy God.'"

[8]Again, the devil taketh him up into an exceeding high mountain, and sheweth him all the kingdoms of the world, and the glory of them; [9]and saith unto him, "All these things will I give thee, if thou wilt fall down and worship me."

[10]Then saith Jesus unto him, "Get thee hence, Satan: for it is written, 'Thou shalt worship the Lord thy God, and him only shalt thou serve.'"

[11]Then the devil leaveth him, and, behold, angels came and ministered unto him.

The Calling of the First Disciples

Mark 1:14-20

Mark 1

Now after that John was put in prison, Jesus came into Galilee, preaching the gospel of the kingdom of God, [15]and saying, "The time is fulfilled, and the kingdom of God is at hand: repent ye, and believe the gospel."

[16]Now as he walked by the sea of Galilee, he saw Simon and Andrew his brother casting a net into the sea: for they were fishers. [17]And Jesus said unto them, "Come ye after me, and I will make you to become fishers of men." [18]And straightway they forsook their nets, and followed him.

[19]And when he had gone a little further thence, he saw James the son of Zebedee, and John his brother, who also were in the ship mending their nets. [20]And straightway he called them: and they left their father Zebedee in the ship with the hired servants, and went after him.

The Marriage at Cana

John 2:1-11

John 2

And the third day there was a marriage in Cana of Galilee; and the mother of Jesus was there: [2]and both Jesus was called, and his disciples, to the marriage. [3]And when they wanted wine, the mother of Jesus saith unto him, "They have no wine."

[4]Jesus saith unto her, "Woman, what have I to do with thee? Mine hour is not yet come."

[5]His mother saith unto the servants, "Whatsoever he saith unto you, do it."

[6]And there were set there six waterpots of stone, after the manner of the purifying of the Jews, containing two or three firkins apiece.

[7]Jesus saith unto them, "Fill the waterpots with water." And they filled them up to the brim.

[8]And he saith unto them, "Draw out now, and bear unto the governor of the feast." And they bare it.

The Marriage Feast at Cana *by Gerard David*

John 2

[9]When the ruler of the feast had tasted the water that was made wine, and knew not whence it was: (but the servants which drew the water knew;) the governor of the feast called the bridegroom, [10]and saith unto him, "Every man at the beginning doth set forth good wine; and when men have well drunk, then that which is worse: but thou hast kept the good wine until now."

[11]This beginning of miracles did Jesus in Cana of Galilee, and manifested forth his glory; and his disciples believed on him.

Jesus and Nicodemus

John 2:23-3:22

John 2

Now when he was in Jerusalem at the passover, in the feast day, many believed in his name, when they saw the miracles which he did. [24]But Jesus did not commit himself unto them, because he knew all men, [25]and needed not that any should testify of man: for he knew what was in man.

John 3

There was a man of the Pharisees named Nicodemus, a ruler of the Jews: [2]the same came to Jesus by night, and said unto him, "Rabbi, we know that thou art a teacher come from God: for no man can do these miracles that thou doest, except God be with him."

[3]Jesus answered and said unto him, "Verily, verily, I say unto thee, except a man be born again, he cannot see the kingdom of God."

[4]Nicodemus saith unto him, "How can a man be born when he is old? Can he enter the second time into his mother's womb, and be born?"

[5]Jesus answered, "Verily, verily, I say unto thee, except a man be born of water and of the Spirit, he cannot enter into the kingdom of God. [6]That which is born of the flesh is flesh; and that which is born of the Spirit is spirit. [7]Marvel

not that I said unto thee, 'Ye must be born again.' [8]The wind bloweth where it listeth, and thou hearest the sound thereof, but canst not tell whence it cometh, and whither it goeth. so is every one that is born of the Spirit."

[9]Nicodemus answered and said unto him, "How can these things be?"

[10]Jesus answered and said unto him, "Art thou a master of Israel, and knowest not these things? [11]Verily, verily, I say unto thee, we speak that we do know, and testify that we have seen; and ye receive not our witness. [12]If I have told you earthly things, and ye believe not, how shall ye believe, if I tell you of heavenly things? [13] And no man hath ascended up to heaven, but he that came down from heaven, even the Son of man which is in heaven. [14]And as Moses lifted up the serpent in the wilderness, even so must the Son of man be lifted up: [15]that whosoever believeth in him should not perish, but have eternal life.

[16]"For God so loved the world, that he gave his only begotten Son, that whosoever believeth in him should not perish, but have everlasting life. [17]For God sent not his Son into the world to condemn the world; but that the world through him might be saved. [18]He that believeth on him is not condemned: but he that believeth not is condemned already, because he hath not believed in the name of the only begotten Son of God. [19]And this is the condemnation, that light is come into the world, and men loved darkness rather than light, because their deeds were evil. [20]For every one that doeth evil hateth the light, neither cometh to the light, lest his deeds should be reproved. [21]But he that doeth truth cometh to the light, that his deeds may be made manifest, that they are wrought in God."

[22]After these things came Jesus and his disciples into the land of Judaea; and there he tarried with them, and baptized.

Jesus and the Woman of Samaria

John 4:1-43

John 4

When therefore the Lord knew how the Pharisees had heard that Jesus made and baptized more disciples than John, [2](though Jesus himself baptized not, but his disciples,) [3]he left Judaea, and departed again into Galilee.

[4]And he must needs go through Samaria. [5]Then cometh he to a city of Samaria, which is called Sychar, near to the parcel of ground that Jacob gave to his son Joseph. [6]Now Jacob's well was there. Jesus therefore, being wearied with his journey, sat thus on the well: and it was about the sixth hour.

[7]There cometh a woman of Samaria to draw water: Jesus saith unto her, "Give me to drink." [8](For his disciples were gone away unto the city to buy meat.)

[9]Then saith the woman of Samaria unto him, "How is it that thou, being a Jew, askest drink of me, when I am a woman of Samaria?" For the Jews have no dealings with the Samaritans.

[10]Jesus answered and said unto her, "If thou knewest the gift of God, and who it is that saith to thee, 'Give me to drink'; thou wouldest have asked of him, and he would have given thee living water."

[11]The woman saith unto him, "Sir, thou hast nothing to draw with, and the well is deep: from whence then hast thou that living water? [12]Art thou greater than our father Jacob, which gave us the well, and drank thereof himself, and his children, and his cattle?"

[13]Jesus answered and said unto her, "Whosoever drinketh of this water shall thirst again: [14]but whosoever drinketh of the water that I shall give him shall never thirst; but the water that I shall give him shall be in him a well of water springing up into everlasting life."

[15]The woman saith unto him, "Sir, give me this water, that I thirst not, neither come hither to draw."

[16]Jesus saith unto her, "Go, call thy husband, and come hither."

John 4

REBECCA AT THE WELL *by Carlo Maratti*

John 4

[17]The woman answered and said, "I have no husband."

Jesus saith unto her, "Thou hast well said, 'I have no husband': [18]for thou hast had five husbands; and he whom thou now hast is not thy husband: in that saidst thou truly."

[19]The woman saith unto him, "Sir, I perceive that thou art a prophet. [20]Our fathers worshipped in this mountain; and ye say, that in Jerusalem is the place where men ought to worship."

[21]Jesus saith unto her, "Woman, believe me, the hour cometh, when ye shall neither in this mountain, nor yet at Jerusalem, worship the Father. [22]Ye worship ye know not what: we know what we worship: for salvation is of the Jews. [23]But the hour cometh, and now is, when the true worshippers shall worship the Father in spirit and in truth: for the Father seeketh such to worship him. [24]God is a Spirit: and they that worship him must worship him in spirit and in truth."

[25]The woman saith unto him, "I know that Messias cometh," which is called Christ: "when he is come, he will tell us all things."

[26]Jesus saith unto her, "I that speak unto thee am he."

[27]And upon this came his disciples, and marvelled that he talked with the woman: yet no man said, "What seekest thou?" or "Why talkest thou with her?"

[28]The woman then left her waterpot, and went her way into the city, and saith to the men [29]"Come, see a man, which told me all things that ever I did: is not this the Christ?" [30]Then they went out of the city, and came unto him.

[31]In the mean while his disciples prayed him, saying, "Master, eat."

[32]But he said unto them, "I have meat to eat that ye know not of."

[33]Therefore said the disciples one to another, "Hath any man brought him aught to eat?"

[34]Jesus saith unto them, "My meat is to do the will of him that sent me, and to finish his work. [35]Say not ye, 'There are yet four months, and then cometh harvest'? Behold, I say unto you, 'Lift up your eyes, and look on the fields; for they are white already to harvest.' [36]And he that reapeth receiveth wages, and gathereth fruit unto life eternal: that both he that soweth and he that reapeth may rejoice together. [37]And herein is that saying true, 'One soweth and another reapeth.' [38]I sent you to reap that whereon ye bestowed no labour: other men laboured, and ye are entered into their labours."

[39]And many of the Samaritans of that city believed on him for the saying of the woman, which testified, "He told me all that ever I did." [40]So when the Samaritans were come unto him, they besought him that he would tarry

John 4

with them: and he abode there two days. [41]And many more believed because of his own word; [42]and said unto the woman, "Now we believe, not because of thy saying: for we have heard him ourselves, and know that this is indeed the Christ, the Saviour of the world."

[43]Now after two days he departed thence, and went into Galilee.

A Healing at Capernaum

Mark 2:1-12

Mark 2

And again he entered into Capernaum after some days; and it was noised that he was in the house. [2]And straightway many were gathered together, insomuch that there was no room to receive them, no, not so much as about the door: and he preached the word unto them. [3]And they come unto him, bringing one sick of the palsy, which was borne of four. [4]And when they could not come nigh unto him for the press, they uncovered the roof where he was: and when they had broken it up, they let down the bed wherein the sick of the palsy lay. [5]When Jesus saw their faith, he said unto the sick of the palsy, "Son, thy sins be forgiven thee."

[6]But there were certain of the scribes sitting there, and reasoning in their hearts, [7]"Why doth this man thus speak blasphemies? Who can forgive sins but God only?"

[8]And immediately when Jesus perceived in his spirit that they so reasoned within themselves, he said unto them, "Why reason ye these things in your hearts? [9]Whether is it easier to say to the sick of the palsy, 'Thy sins be forgiven thee'; or to say, 'Arise, and take up thy bed, and walk'? [10]But that ye may know that the Son of man hath power on earth to forgive sins," (he saith to the sick of the palsy), [11]"I say unto thee, arise, and take up thy bed, and go thy way into thine house." [12]And immediately he arose, took up the bed, and went forth before them all; insomuch that they were all amazed, and glorified God, saying, "We never saw it on this fashion."

THE CALLING OF MATTHEW

MATTHEW 9:9-13

Matthew 9

AND AS JESUS PASSED FORTH FROM THENCE, HE saw a man, named Matthew, sitting at the receipt of custom: and he saith unto him, "Follow me." And he arose, and followed him.

[10]And it came to pass, as Jesus sat at meat in the house, behold, many publicans and sinners came and sat down with him and his disciples. [11]And when the Pharisees saw it, they said unto his disciples, "Why eateth your Master with publicans and sinners?"

[12]But when Jesus heard that, he said unto them, "They that be whole need not a physician, but they that are sick. [13]But go ye and learn what that meaneth, 'I will have mercy, and not sacrifice': for I am not come to call the righteous, but sinners to repentance."

THE CALLING OF ST MATTHEW *by Hendrick Ter Brugghen*

Lord of the Sabbath

Mark 2:23-3:8

Mark 2

AND IT CAME TO PASS, THAT HE WENT THROUGH the corn fields on the sabbath day; and his disciples began, as they went, to pluck the ears of corn. [24]And the Pharisees said unto him, "Behold, why do they on the sabbath day that which is not lawful?"

[25]And he said unto them, "Have ye never read what David did, when he had need, and was an hungred, he, and they that were with him? [26]How he went into the house of God in the days of Abiathar the high priest, and did eat the shewbread, which is not lawful to eat but for the priests, and gave also them which were with him?"

[27]And he said unto them, "The sabbath was made for man, and not man for the sabbath: [28]therefore the Son of man is Lord also of the sabbath."

Mark 3

AND HE ENTERED AGAIN INTO THE SYNAGOGUE; AND THERE was a man there which had a withered hand. [2]And they watched him, whether he would heal him on the sabbath day; that they might accuse him. [3]And he saith unto the man which had the withered hand, "Stand forth."

[4]And he saith unto them, "Is it lawful to do good on the sabbath days, or to do evil? To save life, or to kill?" But they held their peace.

[5]And when he had looked round about on them with anger, being grieved for the hardness of their hearts, he saith unto the man, "Stretch forth thine hand." And he stretched it out: and his hand was restored whole as the other. [6]And the Pharisees went forth, and straightway took counsel with the Herodians against him, how they might destroy him.

[7]But Jesus withdrew himself with his disciples to the sea: and a great multitude from Galilee followed him, and from Judaea, [8]and from Jerusalem, and from Idumaea, and from

Mark 3

beyond Jordan; and they about Tyre and Sidon, a great multitude, when they had heard what great things he did, came unto him.

The Appointment of the Twelve Apostles

Luke 6:12-16

Luke 6

AND IT CAME TO PASS IN THOSE DAYS, THAT HE went out into a mountain to pray, and continued all night in prayer to God. [13]And when it was day, he called unto him his disciples: and of them he chose twelve, whom also he named apostles; [14]Simon, (whom he also named Peter,) and Andrew his brother, James and John, Philip and Bartholomew, [15]Matthew and Thomas, James the son of Alphaeus, and Simon called Zelotes, [16]and Judas the brother of James, and Judas Iscariot, which also was the traitor.

The Sermon on the Mount

Matthew 5:1-16

Matthew 5

AND SEEING THE MULTITUDES, HE WENT UP INTO A mountain: and when he was set, his disciples came unto him: [2]and he opened his mouth, and taught them, saying,

[3]"Blessed are the poor in spirit:
for theirs is the kingdom of heaven.
[4]Blessed are they that mourn:
for they shall be comforted.
[5]Blessed are the meek:
for they shall inherit the earth.

Matthew 5

THE CALLING OF THE SONS OF ZEBEDEE *by Marco Basaiti*

Matthew 5

[6]Blessed are they which do hunger and
thirst after righteousness:
for they shall be filled.
[7]Blessed are the merciful:
for they shall obtain mercy.
[8]Blessed are the pure in heart:
for they shall see God.

Matthew 5

[9]Blessed are the peacemakers:
for they shall be called the children of God.
[10]Blessed are they which are persecuted
for righteousness' sake:
for theirs is the kingdom of heaven.

[11]"Blessed are ye, when men shall revile you, and persecute you, and shall say all manner of evil against you falsely, for my sake. [12]Rejoice, and be exceeding glad: for great is your

THE SERMON ON THE MOUNT AND THE HEALING OF THE LEPER
by Cosimo Rosselli

Matthew 5

reward in heaven: for so persecuted they the prophets which were before you.

[13]"Ye are the salt of the earth: but if the salt have lost his savour, wherewith shall it be salted? It is thenceforth good for nothing, but to be cast out, and to be trodden under foot of men.

[14]"Ye are the light of the world. A city that is set on an hill cannot be hid. [15]Neither do men light a candle, and put it under a bushel, but on a candlestick; and it giveth light unto all that are in the house. [16]Let your light so shine before men, that they may see your good works, and glorify your Father which is in heaven."

"Love Your Enemies"

Matthew 5:43-48

Matthew 5

"Ye have heard that it hath been said, 'Thou shalt love thy neighbour, and hate thine enemy.' [44]But I say unto you, Love your enemies, bless them that curse you, do good to them that hate you, and pray for them which despitefully use you, and persecute you; [45]that ye may be the children of your Father which is in heaven: for he maketh his sun to rise on the evil and on the good, and sendeth rain on the just and on the unjust. [46]For if ye love them which love you, what reward have ye? Do not even the publicans the same? [47]And if ye salute your brethren only, what do ye more than others? Do not even the publicans so? [48]Be ye therefore perfect, even as your Father which is in heaven is perfect."

Treasures in Heaven

Matthew 6:19-34

Matthew 6

"Lay not up for yourselves treasures upon earth, where moth and rust doth corrupt, and where thieves break through and steal: [20]but lay up for yourselves treasures in heaven, where neither moth nor rust doth corrupt, and where thieves do not break through nor steal: [21]for where your treasure is, there will your heart be also.

[22]"The light of the body is the eye: if therefore thine eye be single, thy whole body shall be full of light. [23]But if thine eye be evil, thy whole body shall be full of darkness. If therefore the light that is in thee be darkness, how great is that darkness!

[24]"No man can serve two masters: for either he will hate the one and love the other; or else he will hold to

Matthew 6

the one and despise the other. Ye cannot serve God and mammon.

[25]"Therefore I say unto you, take no thought for your life, what ye shall eat, or what ye shall drink; nor yet for your body, what ye shall put on. Is not the life more than meat, and the body than raiment? [26]Behold the fowls of the air: for they sow not, neither do they reap, nor gather into barns; yet your heavenly Father feedeth them. Are ye not much better than they? [27]Which of you by taking thought can add one cubit unto his stature?

[28]"And why take ye thought for raiment? Consider the lilies of the field, how they grow; they toil not, neither do they spin: [29]and yet I say unto you, that even Solomon in all his glory was not arrayed like one of these. [30]Wherefore, if God so clothe the grass of the field, which to day is, and to morrow is cast into the oven, shall he not much more clothe you, O ye of little faith? [31]Therefore take no thought, saying, 'What shall we eat?' or 'What shall we drink?' or, 'Wherewithal shall we be clothed?' [32](For after all these things do the Gentiles seek:) for your heavenly Father knoweth that ye have need of all these things. [33]But seek ye first the kingdom of God, and his righteousness; and all these things shall be added unto you. [34]Take therefore no thought for the morrow: for the morrow shall take thought for the things of itself. Sufficient unto the day is the evil thereof."

The Centurion's Servant

Luke 7:1-10

Luke 7

NOW WHEN HE HAD ENDED ALL HIS SAYINGS IN the audience of the people, he entered into Capernaum. [2]And a certain centurion's servant, who was dear unto him, was sick, and ready to die. [3]And when he heard of Jesus, he sent unto him the elders of the Jews, beseeching him that he would come and heal his servant. [4]And when they came to Jesus, they besought him instantly, saying, that he

Luke 7

was worthy for whom he should do this: [5]"For he loveth our nation, and he hath built us a synagogue." [6]Then Jesus went with them.

And when he was now not far from the house, the centurion sent friends to him, saying unto him, "Lord, trouble not thyself: for I am not worthy that thou shouldest enter under my roof: [7]wherefore neither thought I myself worthy to come unto thee: but say in a word, and my servant shall be healed. [8]For I also am a man set under authority, having under me soldiers, and I say unto one, 'Go,' and he goeth; and to another, 'Come,' and he cometh: and to my servant, 'Do this,' and he doeth it."

THE CENTURION KNEELS AT THE FEET OF CHRIST *by Joseph-Marie Vien*

Luke 7

[9]When Jesus heard these things, he marvelled at him, and turned him about, and said unto the people that followed him. "I say unto you, I have not found so great faith, no, not in Israel." [10]And they that were sent, returning to the house, found the servant whole that had been sick.

Luke 7

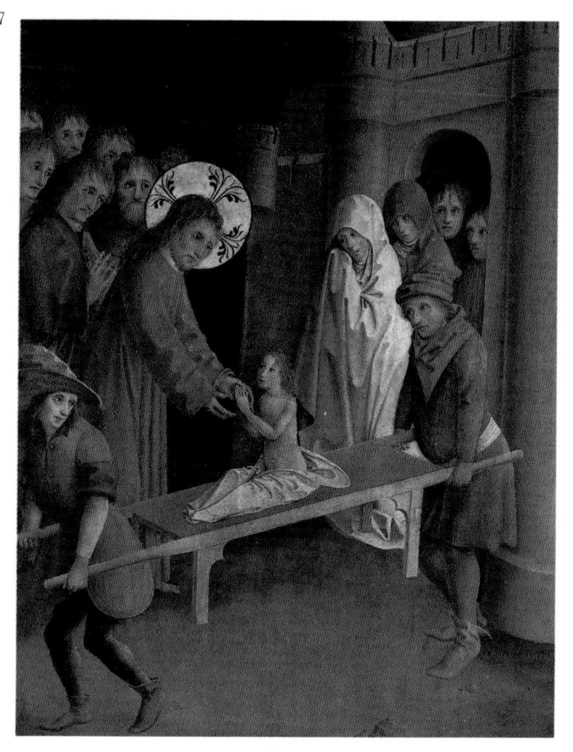

THE RAISING OF THE WIDOW'S SON *by Master of the Darmstädt Passion*

JESUS RAISES A WIDOW'S SON

LUKE 7:11-23

Luke 7

AND IT CAME TO PASS THE DAY AFTER, THAT HE went into a city called Nain; and many of his disciples went with him, and much people. [12]Now when he came nigh to the gate of the city, behold, there was a dead man carried

Luke 7

out, the only son of his mother, and she was a widow: and much people of the city was with her. [13]And when the Lord saw her, he had compassion on her, and said unto her, "Weep not."

[14]And he came and touched the bier: and they that bare him stood still. And he said, "Young man, I say unto thee, Arise." [15]And he that was dead sat up, and began to speak. And he delivered him to his mother.

[16]And there came a fear on all: and they glorified God, saying, that "a great prophet is risen up among us"; and, that "God hath visited his people." [17]And this rumour of him went forth throughout all Judaea, and throughout all the region round about. [18]And the disciples of John shewed him of all these things. [19]And John calling unto him two of his disciples sent them to Jesus, saying, "Art thou he that should come? Or look we for another?"

[20]When the men were come unto him, they said, "John Baptist hath sent us unto thee, saying, 'Art thou he that should come? Or look we for another?'"

[21]And in that same hour he cured many of their infirmities and plagues, and of evil spirits; and unto many that were blind he gave sight. [22]Then Jesus answering said unto them, "Go your way, and tell John what things ye have seen and heard; how that the blind see, the lame walk, the lepers are cleansed, the deaf hear, the dead are raised, to the poor the gospel is preached. [23]And blessed is he, whosoever shall not be offended in me."

The Parable of the Sower

Mark 4:1-20

Mark 4

AND HE BEGAN AGAIN TO TEACH BY THE SEA SIDE: and there was gathered unto him a great multitude, so that he entered into a ship, and sat in the sea; and the whole multitude was by the sea on the land. [2]And he taught them many things by parables, and said unto them in his doctrine, [3]"Hearken; Behold, there went out a sower to sow: [4]and it came to pass, as he sowed, some fell by the way side, and the fowls of the air came and devoured it up. [5]And some fell on stony ground, where it had not much earth; and immediately it sprang up, because it had no depth of earth: [6]but when the sun was up, it was scorched; and because it had no root, it withered away. [7]And some fell among thorns, and the thorns grew up, and choked it, and it yielded no fruit. [8]And other fell on good ground, and did yield fruit that sprang up and increased; and brought forth, some thirty, and some sixty, and some an hundred."

[9]And he said unto them, "He that hath ears to hear, let him hear." [10]And when he was alone, they that were about him with the twelve asked of him the parable. [11]And he

THE PARABLE OF THE SOWER *by Jacopo Bassano*

Mark 4

said unto them, "Unto you it is given to know the mystery of the kingdom of God: but unto them that are without, all these things are done in parables:
[12]"That seeing they may see, and not perceive;
And hearing they may hear, and not understand;
Lest at any time they should be converted,
And their sins should be forgiven them.'"
[13]And he said unto them, "Know ye not this parable? And how then will ye know all parables? [14]The sower soweth the word. [15]And these are they by the way side, where the word is sown; but when they have heard, Satan cometh immediately, and taketh away the word that was sown in their hearts. [16]And these are they likewise which are sown on stony ground; who, when they have heard the word, immediately receive it with gladness; [17]and have no root in themselves, and so endure but for a time: afterward, when affliction or persecution ariseth for the word's sake, immediately they are offended. [18]And these are they which are sown among thorns; such as hear the word, [19]and the cares of this world, and the deceitfulness of riches, and the lusts of other things entering in, choke the word, and it becometh unfruitful. [20]And these are they which are sown on good ground; such as hear the word, and receive it, and bring forth fruit, some thirtyfold, some sixty, and some an hundred."

Parables of the Kingdom (I)

Matthew 13:44-46

Matthew 13

"Again, the kingdom of heaven is like unto treasure hid in a field; the which when a man hath found, he hideth, and for joy thereof goeth and selleth all that he hath, and buyeth that field.

[45]"Again, the kingdom of heaven is like unto a merchant man, seeking goodly pearls; [46]who, when he had found one pearl of great price, went and sold all that he had, and bought it."

Parables of the Kingdom (II)

Mark 4:26-34

Mark 4

AND HE SAID, "SO IS THE KINGDOM OF GOD, AS IF A man should cast seed into the ground; [27]and should sleep, and rise night and day, and the seed should spring and grow up, he knoweth not how. [28]For the earth bringeth forth fruit of herself; first the blade, then the ear, after that the full corn in the ear. [29]But when the fruit is brought forth, immediately he putteth in the sickle, because the harvest is come."

[30]And he said, "Whereunto shall we liken the kingdom of God? Or with what comparison shall we compare it? [31]It is like a grain of mustard seed, which, when it is sown in the earth, is less than all the seeds that be in the earth: [32]but when it is sown, it groweth up, and becometh greater than all herbs, and shooteth out great branches; so that the fowls of the air may lodge under the shadow of it."

[33]And with many such parables spake he the word unto them, as they were able to hear it. [34]But without a parable spake he not unto them: and when they were alone, he expounded all things to his disciples.

Jesus Stills the Storm

Mark 4:35-41

Mark 4

AND THE SAME DAY, WHEN THE EVEN WAS COME, he saith unto them, "Let us pass over unto the other side." [36]And when they had sent away the multitude, they took him even as he was in the ship. And there were also with him other little ships. [37]And there arose a great storm of wind, and the waves beat into the ship, so that it was now full. [38]And he was in the hinder part of the ship, asleep on a pillow: and they awake him, and say unto him, "Master, carest thou not that we perish?"

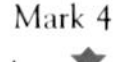

[39]And he arose, and rebuked the wind, and said unto the sea, "Peace, be still." And the wind ceased, and there was a great calm.

[40]And he said unto them, "Why are ye so fearful? How is it that ye have no faith?"

[41]And they feared exceedingly, and said one to another, "What manner of man is this, that even the wind and the sea obey him?"

The Gadarene Swine

Mark 5:1-20

Mark 5

AND THEY CAME OVER UNTO THE OTHER SIDE OF the sea, into the country of the Gadarenes. [2]And when he was come out of the ship, immediately there met him out of the tombs a man with an unclean spirit, [3]who had his dwelling among the tombs; and no man could bind him, no, not with chains: [4]because that he had been often bound with fetters and chains, and the chains had been plucked asunder by him, and the fetters broken in pieces: neither could any man tame him. [5]And always, night and day, he was in the mountains, and in the tombs, crying, and cutting himself with stones.

[6]But when he saw Jesus afar off, he ran and worshipped him, [7]and cried with a loud voice, and said, "What have I to do with thee, Jesus, thou Son of the most high God? I adjure thee by God, that thou torment me not." [8]For he said unto him, "Come out of the man, thou unclean spirit."

[9]And he asked him, "What is thy name?"

And he answered, saying, "My name is Legion: for we are many." [10]And he besought him much that he would not send them away out of the country.

[11]Now there was there nigh unto the mountains a great herd of swine feeding.

[12]And all the devils besought him, saying, "Send us into the swine, that we may enter into them." [13]And forthwith Jesus gave them leave. And the unclean spirits went out,

Mark 5

and entered into the swine; and the herd ran violently down a steep place into the sea, (they were about two thousand;) and were choked in the sea.

[14]And they that fed the swine fled, and told it in the city, and in the country. And they went out to see what it was that was done. [15]And they come to Jesus, and see him that was possessed with the devil, and had the legion, sitting, and clothed, and in his right mind: and they were afraid. [16]And they that saw it told them how it befell to him that was possessed with the devil, and also concerning the swine. [17]And they began to pray him to depart out of their coasts.

[18]And when he was come into the ship, he that had been possessed with the devil prayed him that he might be with him. [19]Howbeit Jesus suffered him not, but saith unto him, "Go home to thy friends, and tell them how great things the Lord hath done for thee, and hath had compassion on thee." [20]And he departed, and began to publish in Decapolis how great things Jesus had done for him: and all men did marvel.

Jairus's Daughter

Mark 5:21-43

Mark 5

And when Jesus was passed over again by ship unto the other side, much people gathered unto him; and he was nigh unto the sea. [22]And, behold, there cometh one of the rulers of the synagogue, Jairus by name; and when he saw him, he fell at his feet, [23]and besought him greatly, saying, "My little daughter lieth at the point of death: I pray thee, come and lay thy hands on her, that she may be healed; and she shall live." [24]And Jesus went with him, and much people followed him, and thronged him.

[25]And a certain woman, which had an issue of blood twelve years, [26]and had suffered many things of many physicians, and had spent all that she had, and was nothing bettered, but rather grew worse, [27]when she had heard of Jesus, came in the press behind, and touched his garment.

Mark 5

THE RAISING OF JAIRUS' DAUGHTER *by George Percy Jacomb-Hood*

Mark 5

[28]For she said, "If I may touch but his clothes, I shall be whole." [29]And straightway the fountain of her blood was dried up; and she felt in her body that she was healed of that plague.

[30]And Jesus, immediately knowing in himself that virtue had gone out of him, turned him about in the press, and said, "Who touched my clothes?"

[31]And his disciples said unto him, "Thou seest the multitude thronging thee, and sayest thou, 'Who touched me?'"

[32]And he looked round about to see her that had done this thing. [33]But the woman fearing and trembling, knowing what was done in her, came and fell down before him, and told him all the truth. [34]And he said unto her, "Daughter, thy faith hath made thee whole; go in peace, and be whole of thy plague."

[35]While he yet spake, there came from the ruler of the synagogue's house certain which said, "Thy daughter is dead: why troublest thou the Master any further?"

[36]As soon as Jesus heard the word that was spoken, he saith unto the ruler of the synagogue, "Be not afraid, only believe."

[37]And he suffered no man to follow him, save Peter, and James, and John the brother of James. [38]And he cometh to

Mark 5

the house of the ruler of the synagogue, and seeth the tumult, and them that wept and wailed greatly. [39]And when he was come in, he saith unto them, "Why make ye this ado, and weep? The damsel is not dead, but sleepeth." [40]And they laughed him to scorn.

But when he had put them all out, he taketh the father and the mother of the damsel, and them that were with him, and entereth in where the damsel was lying. [41]And he took the damsel by the hand, and said unto her, "Talitha cumi"; which is, being interpreted, "Damsel, I say unto thee, arise." [42]And straightway the damsel awoke, and walked; for she was of the age of twelve years. And they were astonished with a great astonishment. [43]And he charged them straitly that no man should know it; and commanded that something should be given her to eat.

Jesus Rejected at Nazareth

Luke 4:16-30

Luke 4

AND HE CAME TO NAZARETH, WHERE HE HAD BEEN brought up; and, as his custom was, he went into the synagogue on the sabbath day, and stood up for to read. [17]And there was delivered unto him the book of the prophet Esaias. And when he had opened the book, he found the place where it was written,

> [18]"The Spirit of the Lord is upon me,
> Because he hath anointed me
> To preach the gospel to the poor;
> He hath sent me to heal the Brokenhearted,
> To preach deliverance to the captives,
> And recovering of sight to the blind,
> To set at liberty them that are bruised,
> [19]To preach the acceptable year of the Lord."

[20]And he closed the book, and he gave it again to the minister, and sat down. And the eyes of all them that were in the synagogue were fastened on him. [21]And he began to say

unto them, "This day is this scripture fulfilled in your ears." Luke 4

[22]And all bare him witness, and wondered at the gracious words which proceeded out of his mouth. And they said, "Is not this Joseph's son?"

[23]And he said unto them, "Ye will surely say unto me this proverb, 'Physician, heal thyself: whatsoever we have heard done in Capernaum, do also here in thy country.'"

[24]And he said, "Verily I say unto you, no prophet is accepted in his own country. [25]But I tell you of a truth, many widows were in Israel in the days of Elias, when the heaven was shut up three years and six months, when great famine was throughout all the land; [26]but unto none of them was Elias sent, save unto Sarepta, a city of Sidon, unto a woman that was a widow. [27]And many lepers were in Israel in the time of Eliseus the prophet; and none of them was cleansed, saving Naaman the Syrian."

[28]And all they in the synagogue, when they heard these things, were filled with wrath, [29]and rose up, and thrust him out of the city, and led him unto the brow of the hill whereon their city was built, that they might cast him down headlong. [30]But he passing through the midst of them went his way.

John the Baptist Beheaded

Mark 6:14-29

Mark 6

And king Herod heard of him (for his name was spread abroad:) and he said, that John the Baptist was risen from the dead, "and therefore mighty works do shew forth themselves in him".

[15]Others said, that "It is Elias. And others said, that "It is a prophet, or as one of the prophets".

[16]But when Herod heard thereof, he said, "It is John, whom I beheaded: he is risen from the dead."

[17]For Herod himself had sent forth and laid hold upon John, and bound him in prison for Herodias' sake, his brother Philip's wife: for he had married her. [18]For John had said unto Herod, "It is not lawful for thee to have thy

Mark 6 brother's wife." [19]Therefore Herodias had a quarrel against him, and would have killed him; but she could not: [20]for Herod feared John, knowing that he was a just man and an holy, and observed him; and when he heard him, he did many things, and heard him gladly.

[21]And when a convenient day was come, that Herod on his birthday made a supper to his lords, high captains, and chief estates of Galilee; [22]and when the daughter of the said Herodias came in, and danced, and pleased Herod and

THE BEHEADING OF JOHN THE BAPTIST *by Maximo Stanzione*

Mark 6 them that sat with him, the king said unto the damsel, "Ask of me whatsoever thou wilt, and I will give it thee." [23]And he sware unto her, "Whatsoever thou shalt ask of me, I will give it thee, unto the half of my kingdom."

[24]And she went forth, and said unto her mother, "What shall I ask?"

And she said, "The head of John the Baptist."

[25]And she came in straightway with haste unto the king, and asked, saying, "I will that thou give me by and by in a charger the head of John the Baptist."

[26]And the king was exceeding sorry; yet for his oath's sake, and for their sakes which sat with him, he would not

John the Baptist Beheaded

Mark 6

Salome with the Head of St John the Baptist *by Andrea Solario*

Mark 6

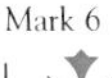

reject her. [27]And immediately the king sent an executioner, and commanded his head to be brought: and he went and beheaded him in the prison, [28]and brought his head in a charger, and gave it to the damsel: and the damsel gave it to her mother. [29]And when his disciples heard of it, they came and took up his corpse, and laid it in a tomb.

The Feeding of the Five Thousand

John 6:1-14

John 6

After these things Jesus went over the sea of Galilee, which is the sea of Tiberias. [2]And a great multitude followed him, because they saw his miracles which he did on them that were diseased. [3]And Jesus went up into a mountain, and there he sat with his disciples. [4]And the passover, a feast of the Jews, was nigh.

[5]When Jesus then lifted up his eyes, and saw a great company come unto him, he saith unto Philip, "Whence shall we buy bread, that these may eat?" [6]And this he said to prove him: for he himself knew what he would do.

[7]Philip answered him, "Two hundred pennyworth of bread is not sufficient for them, that every one of them may take a little."

[8]One of his disciples, Andrew, Simon Peter's brother, saith unto him, [9]"There is a lad here, which hath five barley loaves, and two small fishes: but what are they among so many?"

Christ Preaching on the Sea of Galilee *by Jan Brueghel*

John 6

[10]And Jesus said, "Make the men sit down." Now there was much grass in the place. So the men sat down, in number about five thousand. [11]And Jesus took the loaves; and when he had given thanks, he distributed to the disciples, and the disciples to them that were set down; and likewise of the fishes as much as they would.

[12]When they were filled, he said unto his disciples, "Gather up the fragments that remain, that nothing be lost." [13]Therefore they gathered them together, and filled twelve baskets with the fragments of the five barley loaves, which remained over and above unto them that had eaten.

[14]Then those men, when they had seen the miracle that Jesus did, said, "This is of a truth that prophet that should come into the world."

Jesus Walks on the Water

Matthew 14:22-33

Matthew 14

And straightway Jesus constrained his disciples to get into a ship, and to go before him unto the other side, while he sent the multitudes away. [23]And when he had sent the multitudes away, he went up into a mountain to pray: and when the evening was come, he was there alone. [24]But the ship was now in the midst of the sea, tossed with waves: for the wind was contrary.

[25]And in the fourth watch of the night Jesus went unto them, walking on the sea. [26]And when the disciples saw him walking on the sea, they were troubled, saying, "It is a spirit"; and they cried out for fear.

[27]But straightway Jesus spake unto them, saying, "Be of good cheer; it is I; be not afraid."

[28]And Peter answered him and said, "Lord, if it be thou, bid me come unto thee on the water."

[29]And he said, "Come."

And when Peter was come down out of the ship, he walked on the water, to go to Jesus. [30]But when he saw the

Matthew 14

wind boisterous, he was afraid; and beginning to sink, he cried, saying, "Lord, save me."

[31]And immediately Jesus stretched forth his hand, and caught him, and said unto him, "O thou of little faith, wherefore didst thou doubt?"

[32]And when they were come into the ship, the wind ceased. [33]Then they that were in the ship came and worshipped him, saying, "Of a truth thou art the Son of God."

PETER WALKS ON THE WATER *by Duccio di Buoninsegna*

THE BREAD OF LIFE

JOHN 6:22-40

John 6

THE DAY FOLLOWING, WHEN THE PEOPLE WHICH stood on the other side of the sea saw that there was none other boat there, save that one whereunto his disciples were entered, and that Jesus went not with his disciples into the boat, but that his disciples were gone away alone; [23](howbeit there came other boats from Tiberias nigh unto the place where they did eat bread, after that the Lord had given thanks:) [24]when the people therefore saw that Jesus was not there, neither his disciples, they also took shipping, and came to Capernaum, seeking for Jesus.

[25]And when they had found him on the other side of the sea, they said unto him, "Rabbi, when camest thou hither?"

[26]Jesus answered them and said, "Verily, verily, I say unto you, ye seek me, not because ye saw the miracles, but because ye did eat of the loaves, and were filled. [27]Labour not for the meat which perisheth, but for that meat which endureth unto everlasting life, which the Son of man shall give unto you: for him hath God the Father sealed.

[28]Then said they unto him, "What shall we do, that we might work the works of God?"

[29]Jesus answered and said unto them, "This is the work of God, that ye believe on him whom he hath sent."

[30]They said therefore unto him, "What sign shewest thou then, that we may see, and believe thee? What dost thou work? [31]Our fathers did eat manna in the desert; as it is written. 'He gave them bread from heaven to eat.'"

[32]Then Jesus said unto them, "Verily, verily, I say unto you, Moses gave you not that bread from heaven; but my Father giveth you the true bread from heaven. [33]For the bread of God is he which cometh down from heaven, and giveth life unto the world."

[34]Then said they unto him, "Lord, evermore give us this bread."

[35]And Jesus said unto them, "I am the bread of life: he that cometh to me shall never hunger; and he that believeth on me shall never thirst. [36]But I said unto you, that ye also have seen me, and believe not. [37]All that the Father giveth me shall come to me; and him that cometh to me I will in no wise cast out. [38]For I came down from heaven, not to do mine own will, but the will of him that sent me. [39]And this is the Father's will which hath sent me, that of all which he hath given me I should lose nothing, but should raise it up again at the last day. [40]And this is the will of him that sent me, that every one which seeth the Son, and believeth on him, may have everlasting life: and I will raise him up at the last day."

The Faith of the Woman of Canaan

Matthew 15:21-28

Matthew 15

THEN JESUS WENT THENCE, AND DEPARTED INTO the coasts of Tyre and Sidon. [22]And, behold, a woman of Canaan came out of the same coasts, and cried unto him, saying, "Have mercy on me, O Lord, thou son of David; my daughter is grievously vexed with a devil."

[23]But he answered her not a word. And his disciples came and besought him, saying, "Send her away; for she crieth after us."

[24]But he answered and said, "I am not sent but unto the lost sheep of the house of Israel."

[25]Then came she and worshipped him, saying, "Lord, help me."

[26]But he answered and said, "It is not meet to take the children's bread, and to cast it to the dogs."

[27]And she said, "Truth, Lord: yet the dogs eat of the crumbs which fall from their masters' table."

[28]Then Jesus answered and said unto her, "O woman, great is thy faith: be it unto thee even as thou wilt." And her daughter was made whole from that very hour.

Peter's Confession

Luke 9:18-27

Luke 9

AND IT CAME TO PASS, AS HE WAS ALONE PRAYING, his disciples were with him: and he asked them, saying, "Whom say the people that I am?"

[19]They answering said, "John the Baptist; but some say, Elias; and others say, that one of the old prophets is risen again."

[20]He said unto them, "But whom say ye that I am?"

Peter answering said, "The Christ of God."

[21]And he straitly charged them, and commanded them to tell no man that thing; [22]saying, "The Son of man must

Luke 9

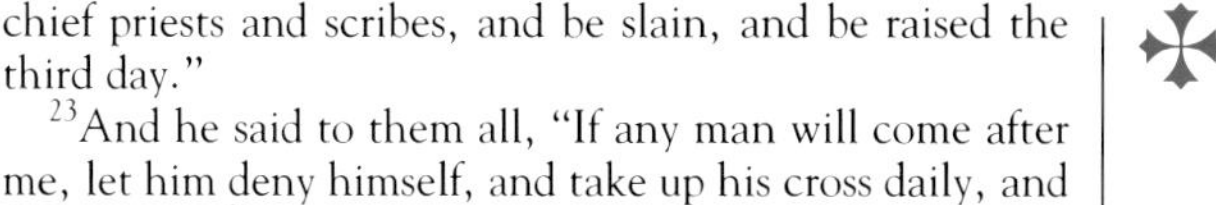

suffer many things, and be rejected of the elders and chief priests and scribes, and be slain, and be raised the third day."

[23]And he said to them all, "If any man will come after me, let him deny himself, and take up his cross daily, and follow me. [24]For whosoever will save his life shall lose it: but whosoever will lose his life for my sake, the same shall save it. [25]For what is a man advantaged, if he gain the whole world, and lose himself, or be cast away? [26]For whosoever shall be ashamed of me and of my words, of him shall the Son of man be ashamed, when he shall come in his own glory, and in his Father's, and of the holy angels. [27]But I tell you of a truth, there be some standing here, which shall not taste of death, till they see the kingdom of God."

The Transfiguration

Matthew 17:1-9

Matthew 17

AND AFTER SIX DAYS JESUS TAKETH PETER, JAMES, and John his brother, and bringeth them up into an high mountain apart, [2]and was transfigured before them: and his face did shine as the sun, and his raiment was white as the light. [3]And, behold, there appeared unto them Moses and Elias talking with him.

[4]Then answered Peter, and said unto Jesus, "Lord, it is good for us to be here: if thou wilt, let us make here three tabernacles: one for thee, and one for Moses, and one for Elias."

[5]While he yet spake, behold, a bright cloud overshadowed them: and behold a voice out of the cloud, which said, "This is my beloved Son, in whom I am well pleased; hear ye him."

[6]And when the disciples heard it, they fell on their face, and were sore afraid. [7]And Jesus came and touched them, and said, "Arise, and be not afraid." [8]And when they had lifted up their eyes, they saw no man, save Jesus only.

Matthew 17

[9]And as they came down from the mountain, Jesus charged them, saying, "Tell the vision to no man, until the Son of man be risen again from the dead."

Jesus Heals a Boy with a Dumb Spirit

Mark 9:14-32

Mark 9

AND WHEN HE CAME TO HIS DISCIPLES, HE SAW A great multitude about them, and the scribes questioning with them. [15]And straightway all the people, when they beheld him, were greatly amazed, and running to him saluted him.

[16]And he asked the scribes, "What question ye with them?"

[17]And one of the multitude answered and said, "Master, I have brought unto thee my son, which hath a dumb spirit; [18]and wheresoever he taketh him, he teareth him: and he foameth, and gnasheth with his teeth, and pineth away: and I spake to thy disciples that they should cast him out; and they could not."

[19]He answereth him, and saith, "O faithless generation, how long shall I be with you? How long shall I suffer you? Bring him unto me."

[20]And they brought him unto him: and when he saw him, straightway the spirit tare him; and he fell on the ground, and wallowed foaming.

[21]And he asked his father, "How long is it ago since this came unto him?"

And he said, "Of a child. [22]And ofttimes it hath cast him into the fire, and into the waters, to destroy him: but if thou canst do any thing, have compassion on us, and help us."

[23]Jesus said unto him, "If thou canst believe, all things are possible to him that believeth."

[24]And straightway the father of the child cried out, and said with tears, "Lord, I believe; help thou mine unbelief."

[25]When Jesus saw that the people came running together, he rebuked the foul spirit, saying unto him, "Thou

Jesus Heals a Boy with a Dumb Spirit

Mark 9

THE TRANSFIGURATION OF CHRIST *by Gentile Bellini*

Mark 9

dumb and deaf spirit, I charge thee, come out of him, and enter no more into him."

[26]And the spirit cried, and rent him sore, and came out of him: and he was as one dead; insomuch that many said, "He is dead." [27]But Jesus took him by the hand, and lifted him up; and he arose.

[28]And when he was come into the house, his disciples asked him privately, "Why could not we cast him out?"

[29]And he said unto them, "This kind can come forth by nothing, but by prayer and fasting."

[30]And they departed thence, and passed through Galilee; and he would not that any man should know it. [31]For he taught his disciples, and said unto them, "The Son of man is delivered into the hands of men, and they shall kill him: and after that he is killed, he shall rise the third day." [32]But they understood not that saying, and were afraid to ask him.

The Greatest in the Kingdom of Heaven

Matthew 18:1-11

Matthew 18

AT THE SAME TIME CAME THE DISCIPLES UNTO Jesus, saying, "Who is the greatest in the kingdom of heaven?"

[2]And Jesus called a little child unto him, and set him in the midst of them, [3]and said, "Verily I say unto you, except ye be converted, and become as little children, ye shall not enter into the kingdom of heaven. [4]Whosoever therefore shall humble himself as this little child, the same is greatest in the kingdom of heaven.

[5]"And whoso shall receive one such little child in my name, receiveth me. [6]But whoso shall offend one of these little ones which believe in me, it were better for him that a milestone were hanged about his neck, and that he were drowned in the depth of the sea.

[7]"Woe unto the world because of offences! For it must needs be that offences come; but woe to that man by whom the offence cometh! [8]Wherefore if thy hand or thy foot offend thee, cut them off, and cast them from thee: it is

Matthew 18

better for thee to enter into life halt or maimed, rather than having two hands or two feet to be cast into everlasting fire. [9]And if thine eye offend thee, pluck it out, and cast it from thee: it is better for thee to enter into life with one eye, rather than having two eyes to be cast into hell fire.

[10]"Take heed that ye despise not one of these little ones; for I say unto you, that in heaven their angels do always behold the face of my Father which is in heaven. [11]For the Son of man is come to save that which was lost."

The Parable of the Unmerciful Servant

Matthew 18:21-19:2

Matthew 18

THEN CAME PETER TO HIM, AND SAID, "LORD, how oft shall my brother sin against me, and I forgive him? Till seven times?"

[22]Jesus saith unto him, "I say not unto thee, 'Until seven times': but, 'Until seventy times seven.'

[23]"Therefore is the kingdom of heaven likened unto a certain king, which would take account of his servants. [24]And when he had begun to reckon, one was brought unto him which owed him ten thousand talents. [25]But forasmuch as he had not to pay, his lord commanded him to be sold, and his wife, and children, and all that he had, and payment to be made.

[26]"The servant therefore fell down, and worshipped him, saying, 'Lord, have patience with me, and I will pay thee all.' [27]Then the lord of that servant was moved with compassion, and loosed him, and forgave him the debt.

[28]"But the same servant went out, and found one of his fellowservants, which owed him an hundred pence: and he laid his hands on him, and took him by the throat, saying, 'Pay me that thou owest.'

[29]"And his fellowservant fell down at his feet, and besought him, saying, 'Have patience with me, and I will pay thee all."

[30]"And he would not: but went and cast him into prison, till he should pay the debt. [31]So when his fellowservants

Matthew 18

saw what was done, they were very sorry, and came and told unto their lord all that was done.

[32]Then his lord, after that he had called him, said unto him, 'O thou wicked servant, I forgave thee all that debt, because thou desiredst me: [33]shouldest not thou also have had compassion on thy fellowservant, even as I had pity on thee?' [34]And his lord was wroth, and delivered him to the tormentors, till he should pay all that was due unto him.

[35]"So likewise shall my heavenly Father do also unto you, if ye from your hearts forgive not every one his brother their trespasses."

Matthew 19

AND IT CAME TO PASS, THAT WHEN JESUS HAD FINISHED these sayings, he departed from Galilee, and came into the coasts of Judaea beyond Jordan; [2]and great multitudes followed him: and he healed them there.

JESUS TEACHES IN THE TEMPLE AT THE FEAST OF TABERNACLES

JOHN 7:37-53

John 7

IN THE LAST DAY, THAT GREAT DAY OF THE FEAST, Jesus stood and cried, saying, "If any man thirst, let him come unto me, and drink. [38]He that believeth on me, as the scripture hath said, out of his belly shall flow rivers of living water." [39](But this spake he of the Spirit, which they that believe on him should receive: for the Holy Ghost was not yet given; because that Jesus was not yet glorified.)

[40]Many of the people therefore, when they heard this saying, said, "Of a truth this is the Prophet."

[41]Others said, "This is the Christ."

But some said, "Shall Christ come out of Galilee? [42]Hath not the scripture said, that Christ cometh of the seed of David, and out of the town of Bethlehem, where David was?" [43]So there was a division among the people because of him. [44]And some of them would have taken him; but no man laid hands on him.

John 7

45 Then came the officers to the chief priests and Pharisees: and they said unto them, "Why have ye not brought him?"

46 The officers answered, "Never man spake like this man."

47 Then answered them the Pharisees, "Are ye also deceived? 48 Have any of the rulers or of the Pharisees believed on him? 49 But this people who knoweth not the law are cursed."

50 Nicodemus saith unto them (he that came to Jesus by night, being one of them,) 51 "Doth our law judge any man, before it hear him, and know what he doeth?"

52 They answered and said unto him, "Art thou also of Galilee? Search, and look: for out of Galilee ariseth no prophet."

53 And every man went unto his own house.

The Woman Taken in Adultery

John 8:1-11

John 8

JESUS WENT UNTO THE MOUNT OF OLIVES. 2 AND EARLY in the morning he came again into the temple, and all the people came unto him; and he sat down, and taught them. 3 And the scribes and Pharisees brought unto him a woman taken in adultery; and when they had set her in the midst, 4 they say unto him, "Master, this woman was taken in adultery, in the very act. 5 Now Moses in the law commanded us, that such should be stoned: but what sayest thou?" 6 This they said, tempting him, that they might have to accuse him.

But Jesus stooped down, and with his finger wrote on the ground, as though he heard them not. 7 So when they continued asking him, he lifted up himself, and said unto them, "He that is without sin among you, let him first cast a stone at her." 8 And again he stooped down, and wrote on the ground.

9 And they which heard it, being convicted by their own conscience, went out one by one, beginning at the eldest,

John 8

THE WOMAN TAKEN IN ADULTERY *by G. B. Benvenuti L'Ortolano*

John 8

even unto the last: and Jesus was left alone, and the woman standing in the midst. [10]When Jesus had lifted up himself, and saw none but the woman, he said unto her, "Woman, where are those thine accusers? Hath no man condemned thee?"

[11]She said, "No man, Lord."

And Jesus said unto her, "Neither do I condemn thee: go, and sin no more."

THE LIGHT OF THE WORLD

JOHN 8:12-20

John 8

THEN SPAKE JESUS AGAIN UNTO THEM, SAYING, "I am the light of the world: he that followeth me shall not walk in darkness, but shall have the light of life."

[13]The Pharisees therefore said unto him, "Thou bearest record of thyself: thy record is not true."

John 8

[14]Jesus answered and said unto them, "Though I bear record of myself, yet my record is true: for I know whence I came, and whither I go; but ye cannot tell whence I come, and whither I go. [15]Ye judge after the flesh; I judge no man. [16]And yet if I judge, my judgment is true: for I am not alone, but I and the Father that sent me. [17]It is also written in your law, that the testimony of two men is true. [18]I am one that bear witness of myself, and the Father that sent me beareth witness of me."

[19]Then said they unto him, "Where is thy Father?"

Jesus answered, "Ye neither know me, nor my Father: if ye had known me, ye should have known my Father also." [20]These words spake Jesus in the temple: and no man laid hands on him; for his hour was not yet come.

Jesus Heals a Man Blind from Birth

John 9

John 9

And as Jesus passed by, he saw a man which was blind from his birth. [2]And his disciples asked him, saying, "Master, who did sin, this man, or his parents, that he was born blind?"

[3]Jesus answered, "Neither hath this man sinned, nor his parents: but that the works of God should be made manifest in him. [4]I must work the works of him that sent me, while it is day: the night cometh, when no man can work. [5]As long as I am in the world, I am the light of the world."

[6]When he had thus spoken, he spat on the ground, and made clay of the spittle, and he anointed the eyes of the blind man with the clay, [7]and said unto him, "Go, wash in the pool of Siloam," (which is by interpretation, Sent.) He went his way therefore, and washed, and came seeing.

[8]The neighbours therefore, and they which before had seen him that he was blind, said, "Is not this he that sat and begged?"

[9]Some said, "This is he", others said, "He is like him"; but he said, "I am he."

[10]Therefore said they unto him, "How were thine eyes opened?"

[11]He answered and said, "A man that is called Jesus made clay, and anointed mine eyes, and said unto me, 'Go to the pool of Siloam, and wash': and I went and washed, and I received sight."

[12]Then said they unto him, "Where is he?"

He said, "I know not."

[13]They brought to the Pharisees him that aforetime was blind. [14]And it was the sabbath day when Jesus made the clay, and opened his eyes. [15]Then again the Pharisees also asked him how he had received his sight. He said unto them, "He put clay upon my eyes, and I washed, and do see."

[16]Therefore said some of the Pharisees, "This man is not of God, because he keepeth not the sabbath day."

Others said, "How can a man that is a sinner do such miracles?" And there was a division among them.

[17]They say unto the blind man again, "What sayest thou of him, that he hath opened thine eyes?"

He said, "He is a prophet."

[18]But the Jews did not believe concerning him, that he had been blind, and received his sight, until they called the parents of him that had received his sight. [19]And they asked them, saying, "Is this your son, who ye say was born blind? How then doth he now see?"

[20]His parents answered them and said, "We know that this is our son, and that he was born blind: [21]but by what means he now seeth, we know not: or who hath opened his eyes, we know not; he is of age; ask him: he shall speak for himself." [22]These words spake his parents, because they feared the Jews: for the Jews had agreed already, that if any man did confess that he was Christ, he should be put out of the synagogue. [23]Therefore said his parents, "He is of age; ask him."

[24]Then again called they the man that was blind, and said unto him, "Give God the praise: we know that this man is a sinner."

[25]He answered and said, "Whether he be a sinner or no, I know not: one thing I know, that, whereas I was blind, now I see."

[26]Then said they to him again, "What did he to thee? How opened he thine eyes?"

Christ Opens the Eyes of a Man *by Duccio di Buoninsegna*

[27]He answered them, "I have told you already, and ye did not hear: wherefore would ye hear it again? Will ye also be his disciples?"

[28]Then they reviled him, and said, "Thou art his disciple; but we are Moses' disciples. [29]We know that God spake unto Moses: as for this fellow, we know not from whence he is."

[30]The man answered and said unto them, "Why herein is a marvellous thing, that ye know not from whence he is, and yet he hath opened mine eyes. [31]Now we know that God heareth not sinners: but if any man be a worshipper of God, and doeth his will, him he heareth. [32]Since the world began was it not heard that any man opened the eyes of one that was born blind. [33]If this man were not of God, he could do nothing."

[34]They answered and said unto him, "Thou wast altogether born in sins, and dost thou teach us?" And they cast him out.

John 9

[35]Jesus heard that they had cast him out; and when he had found him, he said unto him, "Dost thou believe on the Son of God?"

[36]He answered and said, "Who is he, Lord, that I might believe on him?"

[37]And Jesus said unto him, "Thou hast both seen him, and it is he that talketh with thee."

[38]And he said, "Lord, I believe." And he worshipped him.

[39]And Jesus said, "For judgment I am come into this world, that they which see not might see; and that they which see might be made blind."

[40]And some of the Pharisees which were with him heard these words, and said unto him, "Are we blind also?"

[41]Jesus said unto them, "If ye were blind, ye should have no sin: but now ye say, 'We see'; therefore your sin remaineth."

THE GOOD SHEPHERD

JOHN 10:1-21

John 10

"VERILY, VERILY, I SAY UNTO YOU, HE THAT entereth not by the door into the sheepfold, but climbeth up some other way, the same is a thief and a robber. [2]But he that entereth in by the door is the shepherd of the sheep. [3]To him the porter openeth; and the sheep hear his voice: and he calleth his own sheep by name, and leadeth them out. [4]And when he putteth forth his own sheep, he goeth before them, and the sheep follow him: for they know his voice. [5]And a stranger will they not follow, but will flee from him: for they know not the voice of strangers." [6]This parable spake Jesus unto them: but they understood not what things they were which he spake unto them.

[7]Then said Jesus unto them again, "Verily, verily, I say unto you, I am the door of the sheep. [8]All that ever came before me are thieves and robbers: but the sheep did not hear them. [9]I am the door: by me if any man enter in, he

John 10

shall be saved, and shall go in and out, and find pasture. [10]The thief cometh not, but for to steal, and to kill, and to destroy: I am come that they might have life, and that they might have it more abundantly.

[11]"I am the good shepherd: the good shepherd giveth his life for the sheep. [12]But he that is an hireling, and not the shepherd, whose own the sheep are not, seeth the wolf coming, and leaveth the sheep, and fleeth: and the wolf catcheth them, and scattereth the sheep. [13]The hireling fleeth, because he is an hireling, and careth not for the sheep. [14]I am the good shepherd, and know my sheep, and am known of mine. [15]As the Father knoweth me, even so know I the Father: and I lay down my life for the sheep. [16]And other sheep I have, which are not of this fold: them also I must bring, and they shall hear my voice; and there shall be one fold, and one shepherd. [17]Therefore doth my Father love me, because I lay down my life, that I may take it again. [18]No man taketh it from me, but I lay it down of myself. I have power to lay it down, and I have power to take it again. This commandment have I received of my Father."

[19]There was a division therefore again among the Jews for these sayings. [20]And many of them said, "He hath a devil, and is mad; why hear ye him?"

[21]Others said, "These are not the words of him that hath a devil. Can a devil open the eyes of the blind?"

The Parable of the Good Samaritan

Luke 10:25-37

Luke 10

And, behold, a certain lawyer stood up, and tempted him, saying, "Master, what shall I do to inherit eternal life?"

[26]He said unto him, "What is written in the law? How readest thou?"

[27]And he answering said, "Thou shalt love the Lord thy God with all thy heart, and with all thy soul, and with all thy strength, and with all thy mind; and thy neighbour as thyself."

Luke 10

THE PARABLE OF THE GOOD SAMARITAN *by Francesco Bassano*

Luke 10

[28]And he said unto him, "Thou hast answered right: this do, and thou shalt live." [29]But he, willing to justify himself, said unto Jesus, "And who is my neighbour?"

[30]And Jesus answering said, "A certain man went down from Jerusalem to Jericho, and fell among thieves, which stripped him of his raiment, and wounded him, and departed, leaving him half dead. [31]And by chance there came down a certain priest that way: and when he saw him, he passed by on the other side. [32]And likewise a Levite, when he was at the place, came and looked on him, and passed by on the other side. [33]But a certain Samaritan, as he journeyed, came where he was: and when he saw him, he had compassion on him, [34]and went to him, and bound up his wounds, pouring in oil and wine, and set him on his own beast, and brought him to an inn, and took care of him. [35]And on the morrow when he departed, he took out two pence, and gave them to the host, and said unto him, 'Take care of him; and whatsoever thou spendest more, when I come again, I will repay thee.'

[36]"Which now of these three, thinkest thou, was neighbour unto him that fell among the thieves?"

[37]And he said, "He that shewed mercy on him."

Then said Jesus unto him, "Go, and do thou likewise."

Martha and Mary

Luke 10:38-42

Luke 10

NOW IT CAME TO PASS, AS THEY WENT, THAT HE entered into a certain village: and a certain woman named Martha received him into her house. [39]And she had a sister called Mary, which also sat at Jesus' feet, and heard his word. [40]But Martha was cumbered about much serving, and came to him, and said, "Lord, dost thou not care that my sister hath left me to serve alone? Bid her therefore that she help me."

[41]And Jesus answered and said unto her, "Martha, Martha, thou art careful and troubled about many things: [42]but one thing is needful: and Mary hath chosen that good part, which shall not be taken away from her."

The Lord's Prayer

Luke 11:1-13

Luke 11

AND IT CAME TO PASS, THAT, AS HE WAS PRAYING in a certain place, when he ceased, one of his disciples said unto him, "Lord, teach us to pray, as John also taught his disciples."

[2]And he said unto them, "When ye pray, say,

"'Our Father which art in heaven,
Hallowed be thy name.
Thy kingdom come.
Thy will be done, as in heaven, so in earth.
[3]Give us day by day our daily bread.
[4]And forgive us our sins;
For we also forgive every one that is indebted to us.
And lead us not into temptation;
But deliver us from evil.'"

Luke 11

[5]And he said unto them, "Which of you shall have a friend, and shall go unto him at midnight, and say unto him, 'Friend, lend me three loaves; [6]for a friend of mine in his journey is come to me, and I have nothing to set before him?'

[7]"And he from within shall answer and say, 'Trouble me not: the door is now shut, and my children are with me in bed; I cannot rise and give thee.' [8]I say unto you, though he will not rise and give him, because he is his friend, yet because of his importunity he will rise and give him as many as he needeth.

[9]"And I say unto you, ask, and it shall be given you; seek, and ye shall find; knock, and it shall be opened unto you. [10]For every one that asketh receiveth; and he that seeketh findeth; and to him that knocketh it shall be opened.

[11]"If a son shall ask bread of any of you that is a father, will he give him a stone? Or if he ask a fish, will he for a fish give him a serpent? [12]Or if he shall ask an egg, will he offer him a scorpion? [13]If ye then, being evil, know how to give good gifts unto your children: how much more shall your heavenly Father give the Holy Spirit to them that ask him?"

The Strait Gate

Luke 13:22-35

Luke 13

AND HE WENT THROUGH THE CITIES AND VILlages, teaching, and journeying toward Jerusalem. [23]Then said one unto him, "Lord, are there few that be saved?"

And he said unto them, [24]"Strive to enter in at the strait gate: for many, I say unto you, will seek to enter in, and shall not be able. [25]When once the master of the house is risen up, and hath shut to the door, and ye begin to stand without, and to knock at the door, saying,

The Good Being Led to Heaven *by Rogier van der Weyden*

Luke 13

'Lord, Lord, open unto us'; and he shall answer and say unto you, 'I know you not whence ye are': [26]then shall ye begin to say, 'We have eaten and drunk in thy presence, and thou hast taught in our streets.'

[27]"But he shall say, 'I tell you, I know you not whence ye are; depart from me, all ye workers of iniquity.'

[28]"There shall be weeping and gnashing of teeth, when ye shall see Abraham, and Isaac, and Jacob, and all the prophets, in the kingdom of God, and you yourselves thrust out. [29]And they shall come from the east, and from the west, and from the north, and from the south, and shall sit down in the kingdom of God. [30]And, behold, there are last which shall be first, and there are first which shall be last."

[31]The same day there came certain of the Pharisees, saying unto him, "Get thee out, and depart hence: for Herod will kill thee."

[32]And he said unto them, "Go ye, and tell that fox, 'Behold, I cast out devils, and I do cures to day and to morrow, and the third day I shall be perfected.' [33]Nevertheless I must walk to day, and to morrow, and the day following: for it cannot be that a prophet perish out of Jerusalem.

[34]"O Jerusalem, Jerusalem, which killest the prophets, and stonest them that are sent unto thee; how often would I have gathered thy children together, as a hen doth gather her brood under her wings, and ye would not! [35]Behold, your house is left unto you desolate: and verily I say unto you, ye shall not see me, until the time come when ye shall say, 'Blessed is he that cometh in the name of the Lord.'"

The Parable of the Great Banquet

Luke 14:1-24

Luke 14

AND IT CAME TO PASS, AS HE WENT INTO THE house of one of the chief Pharisees to eat bread on the sabbath day, that they watched him. [2]And, behold, there was a certain man before him which had the dropsy. [3]And

Jesus answering spake unto the lawyers and Pharisees, saying, "Is it lawful to heal on the sabbath day?" [4]And they held their peace.

And he took him, and healed him, and let him go; [5]and answered them, saying, "Which of you shall have an ass or an ox fallen into a pit, and will not straightway pull him out on the sabbath day?" [6]And they could not answer him again to these things.

[7]And he put forth a parable to those which were bidden, when he marked how they chose out the chief rooms; saying unto them, [8]"When thou art bidden of any man to a wedding, sit not down in the highest room; lest a more honourable man than thou be bidden of him; [9]and he that bade thee and him come and say to thee, 'Give this man place'; and thou begin with shame to take the lowest room. [10]But when thou art bidden, go and sit down in the lowest room; that when he that bade thee cometh, he may say unto thee, 'Friend, go up higher': then shalt thou have worship in the presence of them that sit at meat with thee. [11]For whosoever exalteth himself shall be abased; and he that humbleth himself shall be exalted."

[12]Then said he also to him that bade him, "When thou makest a dinner or a supper, call not thy friends, nor thy brethren, neither thy kinsmen, nor thy rich neighbours; lest they also bid thee again, and a recompence be made thee. [13]But when thou makest a feast, call the poor, the maimed, the lame, the blind: [14]and thou shalt be blessed; for they cannot recompense thee: for thou shalt be recompensed at the resurrection of the just."

[15]And when one of them that sat at meat with him heard these things, he said unto him, "Blessed is he that shall eat bread in the kingdom of God."

[16]Then said he unto him, "A certain man made a great supper, and bade many: [17]and sent his servant at supper time to say to them that were bidden, 'Come; for all things are now ready.'

[18]"And they all with one consent began to make excuse. The first said unto him, 'I have bought a piece of ground, and I must needs go and see it: I pray thee have me excused.'

[19]"And another said, 'I have bought five yoke of oxen, and I go to prove them: I pray thee have me excused.'

Luke 14

[20]"And another said, 'I have married a wife, and therefore I cannot come.'

[21]"So that servant came, and shewed his lord these things. Then the master of the house being angry said to his servant, 'Go out quickly into the streets and lanes of the city, and bring in hither the poor, and the maimed, and the halt, and the blind.'

[22]"And the servant said, 'Lord, it is done as thou hast commanded, and yet there is room.'

[23]"And the lord said unto the servant, 'Go out into the highways and hedges, and compel them to come in, that my house may be filled. [24]For I say unto you, that none of those men which were bidden shall taste of my supper.'"

The Parables of the Lost Sheep and the Lost Coin

Luke 15:1-10

Luke 15

THEN DREW NEAR UNTO HIM ALL THE PUBLICANS and sinners for to hear him. [2]And the Pharisees and scribes murmured, saying, "This man receiveth sinners, and eateth with them."

[3]And he spake this parable unto them, saying, [4]"What man of you, having an hundred sheep, if he lose one of them doth not leave the ninety and nine in the wilderness, and go after that which is lost, until he find it? [5]And when he hath found it, he layeth it on his shoulders, rejoicing. [6]And when he cometh home, he calleth together his friends and neighbours, saying unto them, 'Rejoice with me; for I have found my sheep which was lost.' [7]I say unto you, that likewise joy shall be in heaven over one sinner that repenteth, more than over ninety and nine just persons, which need no repentance.

[8]"Either what woman having ten pieces of silver, if she lose one piece, doth not light a candle, and sweep the house, and seek diligently till she find it? [9]And when she hath found it, she calleth her friends and her neighbours together, saying, 'Rejoice with me; for I have found the

Luke 15

piece which I had lost.' [10]Likewise, I say unto you, there is joy in the presence of the angels of God over one sinner that repenteth."

The Parable of the Prodigal Son

Luke 15:11-32

Luke 15

And he said, "A certain man had two sons: [12]and the younger of them said to his father, 'Father, give me the portion of goods that falleth to me.' And he divided unto them his living.

[13]"And not many days after the younger son gathered all together, and took his journey into a far country, and there wasted his substance with riotous living. [14]And when he had spent all, there arose a mighty famine in that land; and he began to be in want. [15]And he went and joined himself to a citizen of that country; and he sent him into his fields to feed swine. [16]And he would fain have filled his belly with the husks that the swine did eat: and no man gave unto him.

[17]"And when he came to himself, he said, 'How many hired servants of my father's have bread enough and to spare, and I perish with hunger! [18]I will arise and go to my father, and will say unto him, "Father, I have sinned against heaven, and before thee, [19]and am no more worthy to be called thy son: make me as one of thy hired servants."' [20]And he arose, and came to his father.

But when he was yet a great way off, his father saw him, and had compassion, and ran, and fell on his neck, and kissed him.

[21]"And the son said unto him, 'Father, I have sinned against heaven, and in thy sight, and am no more worthy to be called thy son.'

[22]"But the father said to his servants, 'Bring forth the best robe, and put it on him; and put a ring on his hand, and shoes on his feet: [23]And bring hither the fatted calf, and kill it; and let us eat, and be merry: [24]for this my son was dead, and is alive again; he was lost, and is found.' And they began to be merry.

[25]"Now his elder son was in the field: and as he came and drew nigh to the house, he heard musick and dancing. [26]And he called one of the servants, and asked what these things meant. [27]And he said unto him, 'Thy brother is come; and thy father hath killed the fatted calf, because he hath received him safe and sound.'

[28]"And he was angry, and would not go in: therefore came his father out, and entreated him. [29]And he answering said to his father, 'Lo, these many years do I serve thee, neither transgressed I at any time thy commandment: and yet thou never gavest me a kid, that I might make merry

The Return of the Prodigal Son *by Rembrandt*

Luke 15

with my friends: [30]but as soon as this thy son was come, which hath devoured thy living with harlots, thou hast killed for him the fatted calf.'

[31]"And he said unto him, 'Son, thou art ever with me, and all that I have is thine. [32]It was meet that we should make merry, and be glad: for this thy brother was dead, and is alive again; and was lost, and is found.'"

THE PARABLE OF THE RICH MAN AND LAZARUS

LUKE 16:19-31

Luke 16

"THERE WAS A CERTAIN RICH MAN, WHICH was clothed in purple and fine linen, and fared sumptuously every day: [20]and there was a certain beggar named Lazarus, which was laid at his gate, full of sores, [21]and desiring to be fed with the crumbs which fell from the rich man's table: moreover the dogs came and licked his sores.

[22]"And it came to pass, that the beggar died, and was carried by the angels into Abraham's bosom: the rich man also died, and was buried; [23]and in hell he lift up his eyes, being in torments, and seeth Abraham afar off, and Lazarus in his bosom. [24]And he cried and said, 'Father Abraham, have mercy on me, and send Lazarus, that he may dip the tip of his finger in water, and cool my tongue; for I am tormented in this flame.'

[25]"But Abraham said, 'Son, remember that thou in thy lifetime receivedst thy good things, and likewise Lazarus evil things: but now he is comforted, and thou art tormented. [26]And beside all this, between us and you there is a great gulf fixed: so that they which would pass from hence to you cannot; neither can they pass to us, that would come from thence.'

[27]"Then he said, 'I pray thee therefore, father, that thou wouldest send him to my father's house: [28]for I have five brethren; that he may testify unto them, lest they also come into this place of torment.'

[29]"Abraham saith unto him, 'They have Moses and the prophets; let them hear them.'

Luke 16

THE RICH MAN AND LAZARUS *by Bonifacio de' Pitati*

Luke 16

[30]"And he said, 'Nay, father Abraham: but if one went unto them from the dead, they will repent.'

[31]"And he said unto him, 'If they hear not Moses and the prophets, neither will they be persuaded, though one rose from the dead.'"

THE PARABLE OF THE PHARISEE AND THE PUBLICAN

LUKE 18:9-14

Luke 18

AND HE SPAKE THIS PARABLE UNTO CERTAIN which trusted in themselves that they were righteous, and despised others: [10]"Two men went up into the temple to pray; the one a Pharisee, and the other a publican. [11]The Pharisee stood and prayed thus with himself, 'God, I thank thee, that I am not as other men are, extortioners, unjust, adulterers, or even as this publican. [12]I fast twice in the week, I give tithes of all that I possess.'

[13]"And the publican, standing afar off, would not lift up so much as his eyes unto heaven, but smote upon his breast, saying, 'God be merciful to me a sinner.'

[14]"I tell you, this man went down to his house justified rather than the other: for every one that exalteth himself shall be abased; and he that humbleth himself shall be exalted."

Jesus Blesses Little Children

Mark 10:13-16

Mark 10

AND THEY BROUGHT YOUNG CHILDREN TO HIM, that he should touch them: and his disciples rebuked those that brought them. [14]But when Jesus saw it, he was much displeased, and said unto them, "Suffer the little children to come unto me, and forbid them not: for of such is the kingdom of God. [15]Verily I say unto you, whosoever shall not receive the kingdom of God as a little child, he shall not enter therein." [16]And he took them up in his arms, put his hands upon them, and blessed them.

The Rich Young Man

Mark 10:17-31

Mark 10

AND WHEN HE WAS GONE FORTH INTO THE WAY, there came one running, and kneeled to him, and asked him, "Good Master, what shall I do that I may inherit eternal life?"

[18]And Jesus said unto him, "Why callest thou me good? There is none good but one, that is, God. [19]Thou knowest the commandments, 'Do not commit adultery, Do not kill, Do not steal, Do not bear false witness, Defraud not, Honour thy father and mother.'"

[20]And he answered and said unto him, "Master, all these have I observed from my youth."

[21]Then Jesus beholding him loved him, and said unto him, "One thing thou lackest: go thy way, sell whatsoever thou hast, and give to the poor, and thou shalt have treasure in heaven: and come take up the cross, and follow me."

[22]And he was sad at that saying, and went away grieved: for he had great possessions.

Mark 10

[23]And Jesus looked round about, and saith unto his disciples, "How hardly shall they that have riches enter into the kingdom of God!"

[24]And the disciples were astonished at his words. But Jesus answereth again, and saith unto them, "Children, how hard is it for them that trust in riches to enter into the kingdom of God! [25]It is easier for a camel to go through the eye of a needle, than for a rich man to enter into the kingdom of God."

[26]And they were astonished out of measure, saying among themselves, "Who then can be saved?"

[27]And Jesus looking upon them saith, "With men it is impossible, but not with God: for with God all things are possible."

[28]Then Peter began to say unto him, "Lo, we have left all, and have followed thee."

[29]And Jesus answered and said, "Verily I say unto you, there is no man that hath left house, or brethren, or sisters, or father, or mother, or wife, or children, or lands, for my sake, and the gospel's, [30]but he shall receive an hundredfold now in this time, houses, and brethren, and sisters, and mothers, and children, and lands, with persecutions; and in the world to come eternal life. [31]But many that are first shall be last; and the last first."

The Parable of the Labourers in the Vineyard

Matthew 20:1-16

Matthew 20

"For the kingdom of heaven is like unto a man that is an householder, which went out early in the morning to hire labourers into his vineyard. [2]And when he had agreed with the labourers for a penny a day, he sent them into his vineyard.

[3]"And he went out about the third hour, and saw others standing idle in the marketplace, [4]and said unto them: 'Go ye also into the vineyard, and whatsoever is right I will give you.' And they went their way.

Matthew 20

[5]"Again he went out about the sixth and ninth hour, and did likewise. [6]And about the eleventh hour he went out, and found others standing idle, and saith unto them, 'Why stand ye here all the day idle?'

[7]"They say unto him, 'Because no man hath hired us.'

He saith unto them, 'Go ye also into the vineyard; and whatsoever is right, that shall ye receive.'

[8]"So when even was come, the lord of the vineyard saith unto his steward, 'Call the labourers, and give them their hire, beginning from the last unto the first.'

[9]"And when they came that were hired about the eleventh hour, they received every man a penny. [10]But when the first came, they supposed that they should have received more; and they likewise received every man a penny. [11]And when they had received it, they murmured against the goodman of the house, [12]saying, 'These last have wrought but one hour, and thou hast made them equal unto us, which have borne the burden and heat of the day.'

[13]"But he answered one of them, and said, 'Friend, I do thee no wrong: didst not thou agree with me for a penny? [14]Take that thine is, and go thy way: I will give unto this last, even as unto thee. [15]Is it not lawful for me to do what I will with mine own? Is thine eye evil, because I am good?'

[16]"So the last shall be first, and the first last: for many be called, but few chosen."

Blind Bartimaeus

Mark 10:46-52

Mark 10

AND THEY CAME TO JERICHO: AND AS HE WENT OUT of Jericho with his disciples and a great number of people, blind Bartimaeus, the son of Timaeus, sat by the highway side begging. [47]And when he heard that it was Jesus of Nazareth, he began to cry out, and say, "Jesus, thou son of David, have mercy on me."

Mark 10

48 And many charged him that he should hold his peace: but he cried the more a great deal, "Thou son of David, have mercy on me."

49 And Jesus stood still, and commanded him to be called. And they call the blind man, saying unto him, "Be of good comfort, rise; he calleth thee." 50 And he, casting away his garment, rose, and came to Jesus.

51 And Jesus answered and said unto him, "What wilt thou that I should do unto thee?"

The blind man said unto him, "Lord, that I might receive my sight."

52 And Jesus said unto him, "Go thy way; thy faith hath made thee whole." And immediately he received his sight, and followed Jesus in the way.

Zacchaeus

Luke 19:2-10

Luke 19

AND, BEHOLD, THERE WAS A MAN NAMED Zacchaeus, which was the chief among the publicans, and he was rich. 3 And he sought to see Jesus who he was; and could not for the press, because he was little of stature. 4 And he ran before, and climbed up into a sycomore tree to see him: for he was to pass that way.

5 And when Jesus came to the place, he looked up, and saw him, and said unto him, "Zacchaeus, make haste, and come down; for to day I must abide at thy house." 6 And he made haste, and came down, and received him joyfully.

7 And when they saw it, they all murmured, saying, that he was "gone to be guest with a man that is a sinner".

8 And Zacchaeus stood, and said unto the Lord; "Behold, Lord, the half of my goods I give to the poor; and if I have taken any thing from any man by false accusation, I restore him fourfold."

9 And Jesus said unto him, "This day is salvation come to this house, forsomuch as he also is a son of Abraham. 10 For the Son of man is come to seek and to save that which was lost."

The Raising of Lazarus

John 11

Now a certain man was sick, named Lazarus, of Bethany, the town of Mary and her sister Martha. [2](It was that Mary which anointed the Lord with ointment, and wiped his feet with her hair, whose brother Lazarus was sick.) [3]Therefore his sisters sent unto him, saying, "Lord, behold, he whom thou lovest is sick."

[4]When Jesus heard that, he said, "This sickness is not unto death, but for the glory of God, that the Son of God might be glorified thereby." [5]Now Jesus loved Martha, and

The Resurrection of Lazarus, *French School*

her sister, and Lazarus. [6]When he had heard therefore that he was sick, he abode two days still in the same place where he was.

[7]Then after that saith he to his disciples, "Let us go into Judaea again."

[8]His disciples say unto him, "Master, the Jews of late sought to stone thee; and goest thou thither again?"

[9]Jesus answered, "Are there not twelve hours in the day? If any man walk in the day, he stumbleth not, because he

seeth the light of this world. [10]But if a man walk in the night, he stumbleth, because there is no light in him."

[11]These things said he: and after that he saith unto them, "Our friend Lazarus sleepeth; but I go, that I may awake him out of sleep."

[12]Then said his disciples, "Lord, if he sleep, he shall do well." [13]Howbeit Jesus spake of his death: but they thought that he had spoken of taking of rest in sleep.

[14]Then said Jesus unto them plainly, "Lazarus is dead. [15]And I am glad for your sakes that I was not there, to the intent ye may believe; nevertheless let us go unto him."

[16]Then said Thomas, which is called Didymus, unto his fellow disciples, "Let us also go, that we may die with him."

[17]Then when Jesus came, he found that he had lain in the grave four days already. [18]Now Bethany was nigh unto Jerusalem, about fifteen furlongs off: [19]and many of the Jews came to Martha and Mary, to comfort them concerning their brother. [20]Then Martha, as soon as she heard that Jesus was coming, went and met him: but Mary sat still in the house.

[21]Then said Martha unto Jesus, "Lord, if thou hadst been here, my brother had not died. [22]But I know, that even now, whatsoever thou wilt ask of God, God will give it thee."

[23]Jesus saith unto her, "Thy brother shall rise again."

[24]Martha saith unto him, "I know that he shall rise again in the resurrection at the last day."

[25]Jesus said unto her, "I am the resurrection, and the life: he that believeth in me, though he were dead, yet shall he live: [26]and whosoever liveth and believeth in me shall never die. Believest thou this?"

[27]She saith unto him, "Yea, Lord: I believe that thou art the Christ, the Son of God, which should come into the world."

[28]And when she had so said, she went her way, and called Mary her sister secretly, saying, "The Master is come, and calleth for thee." [29]As soon as she heard that, she arose quickly, and came unto him. [30]Now Jesus was not yet come into the town, but was in that place where Martha met him. [31]The Jews then which were with her in the house, and comforted her, when they saw Mary, that

she rose up hastily and went out, followed her, saying, "She goeth unto the grave to weep there."

[32]Then when Mary was come where Jesus was, and saw him, she fell down at his feet, saying unto him, "Lord, if thou hadst been here, my brother had not died."

[33]When Jesus therefore saw her weeping, and the Jews also weeping which came with her, he groaned in the spirit, and was troubled, [34]and said, "Where have ye laid him?"

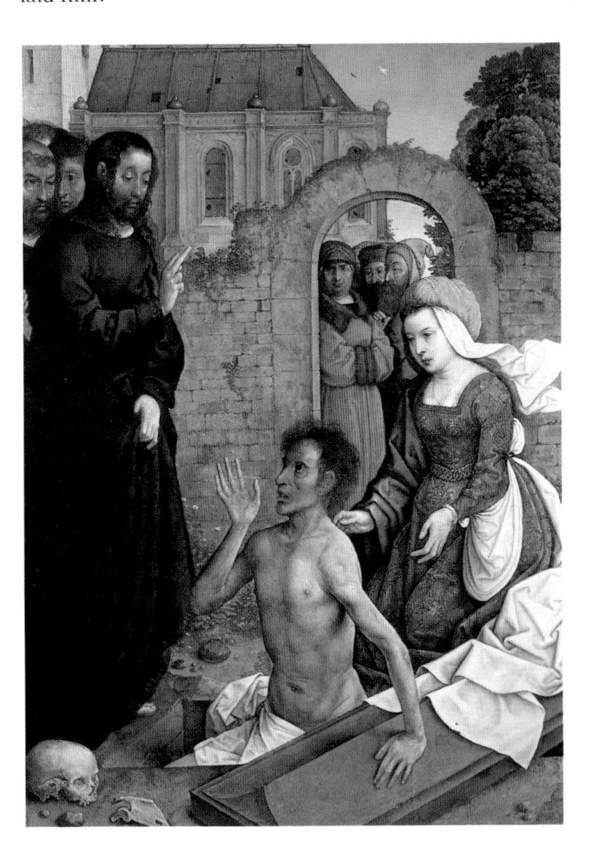

THE RESURRECTION OF LAZARUS *by Juan de Flandres*

They said unto him, "Lord, come and see."

[35]Jesus wept.

[36]Then said the Jews, "Behold how he loved him!"

[37]And some of them said, "Could not this man, which opened the eyes of the blind, have caused that even this man should not have died?"

[38]Jesus therefore again groaning in himself cometh to the grave. It was a cave, and a stone lay upon it. [39]Jesus said, "Take ye away the stone."

Martha, the sister of him that was dead, saith unto him, "Lord, by this time he stinketh: for he hath been dead four days."

[40]Jesus saith unto her, "Said I not unto thee, that, if thou wouldest believe, thou shouldest see the glory of God?"

[41]Then they took away the stone from the place where the dead was laid. And Jesus lifted up his eyes, and said, "Father, I thank thee that thou hast heard me. [42]And I knew that thou hearest me always: but because of the people which stand by I said it, that they may believe that thou hast sent me."

[43]And when he thus had spoken, he cried with a loud voice, "Lazarus, come forth." [44]And he that was dead came forth, bound hand and foot with graveclothes: and his face was bound about with a napkin.

Jesus saith unto them, "Loose him, and let him go."

[45]Then many of the Jews which came to Mary, and had seen the things which Jesus did, believed on him. [46]But some of them went their ways to the Pharisees, and told them what things Jesus had done.

[47]Then gathered the chief priests and the Pharisees a council, and said, "What do we? For this man doeth many miracles. [48]If we let him thus alone, all men will believe on him: and the Romans shall come and take away both our place and nation."

[49]And one of them, named Caiaphas, being the high priest that same year, said unto them, "Ye know nothing at all, [50]nor consider that it is expedient for us, that one man should die for the people, and that the whole nation perish not."

[51]And this spake he not of himself: but being high priest that year, he prophesied that Jesus should die for that nation; [52]and not for that nation only, but that also he

John 11

should gather together in one the children of God that were scattered abroad. [53]Then from that day forth they took counsel together for to put him to death.

[54]Jesus therefore walked no more openly among the Jews; but went thence unto a country near to the wilderness, into a city called Ephraim, and there continued with his disciples.

[55]And the Jews' passover was nigh at hand: and many went out of the country up to Jerusalem before the Passover, to purify themselves. [56]Then sought they for Jesus, and spake among themselves, as they stood in the temple, "What think ye, that he will not come to the feast?"

[57]Now both the chief priests and the Pharisees had given a commandment, that, if any man knew where he were, he should shew it, that they might take him.

Jesus Anointed at Bethany

John 12:1-13

John 12

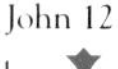

THEN JESUS SIX DAYS BEFORE THE PASSOVER came to Bethany, where Lazarus was which had been dead, whom he raised from the dead. [2]There they made him a supper; and Martha served: but Lazarus was one of them that sat at the table with him. [3]Then took Mary a pound of ointment of spikenard, very costly, and anointed the feet of Jesus, and wiped his feet with her hair: and the house was filled with the odour of the ointment.

[4]Then saith one of his disciples, Judas Iscariot, Simon's son, which should betray him, [5]"Why was not this ointment sold for three hundred pence, and given to the poor?" [6]This he said, not that he cared for the poor; but because he was a thief, and had the bag, and bare what was put therein.

[7]Then said Jesus, "Let her alone: against the day of my burying hath she kept this. [8]For the poor always ye have with you; but me ye have not always."

John 12

[9]Much people of the Jews therefore knew that he was there: and they came not for Jesus' sake only, but that they might see Lazarus also, whom he had raised from the dead. [10]But the chief priests consulted that they might put Lazarus also to death; [11]because that by reason of him many of the Jews went away, and believed on Jesus.

[12]On the next day much people that were come to the feast, when they heard that Jesus was coming to Jerusalem, [13]took branches of palm trees, and went forth to meet him, and cried, "Hosanna: Blessed is the King of Israel that cometh in the name of the Lord."

The Triumphal Entry

Luke 19:29-44

Luke 19

AND IT CAME TO PASS, WHEN HE WAS COME NIGH to Bethphage and Bethany, at the mount called the mount of Olives, he sent two of his disciples, [30]saying, "Go ye into the village over against you; in the which at your entering ye shall find a colt tied, whereon yet never man sat: loose him, and bring him hither. [31]And if any man ask you, 'Why do ye loose him?' thus shall ye say unto him, 'Because the Lord hath need of him.'"

[32]And they that were sent went their way, and found even as he had said unto them. [33]And as they were loosing the colt, the owners thereof said unto them, "Why loose ye the colt?"

[34]And they said, "The Lord hath need of him."

[35]And they brought him to Jesus: and they cast their garments upon the colt, and they set Jesus thereon. [36]And as he went, they spread their clothes in the way.

[37]And when he was come nigh, even now at the descent of the mount of Olives, the whole multitude of the disciples began to rejoice and praise God with a loud voice for all the mighty works that they had seen; [38]saying, "Blessed be the King that cometh in the name of the Lord: peace in heaven, and glory in the highest."

ENTRY INTO JERUSALEM *by Duccio di Buoninsegna*

Luke 19

[39]And some of the Pharisees from among the multitude said unto him, "Master, rebuke thy disciples."

[40]And he answered and said unto them, "I tell you that, if these should hold their peace, the stones would immediately cry out."

[41]And when he was come near, he beheld the city, and wept over it, [42]saying, "If thou hadst known, even thou, at least in this thy day, the things which belong unto thy peace! But now they are hid from thine eyes. [43]For the days shall come upon thee, that thine enemies shall cast a trench about thee, and compass thee round, and keep thee in on every side, [44]and shall lay thee even with the ground, and thy children within thee; and they shall not leave in thee one stone upon another; because thou knewest not the time of thy visitation."

The Cleansing of the Temple

Matthew 21:12-17

Matthew 21

And Jesus went into the temple of God, and cast out all them that sold and bought in the temple, and overthrew the tables of the moneychangers, and the seats of them that sold doves, [13]and said unto them, "It is written, 'My house shall be called the house of prayer'; but ye have made it a 'den of thieves'."

[14]And the blind and the lame came to him in the temple; and he healed them. [15]And when the chief priests and scribes saw the wonderful things that he did, and the children crying in the temple, and saying, "Hosanna to the son of David"; they were sore displeased, [16]and said unto him, "Hearest thou what these say?"

And Jesus saith unto them, "Yea, have ye never read, 'Out of the mouth of babes and sucklings thou hast perfected praise'?"

[17]And he left them, and went out of the city into Bethany; and he lodged there.

Matthew 21

THE CLEANSING OF THE TEMPLE *by Ambrogio Bondone Giotto*

THE AUTHORITY OF JESUS QUESTIONED

LUKE 20:1-8

Luke 20

AND IT CAME TO PASS, THAT ON ONE OF THOSE days, as he taught the people in the temple, and preached the gospel, the chief priests and the scribes came upon him with the elders, [2]and spake unto him, saying, "Tell us, by what authority doest thou these things? Or who is he that gave thee this authority?"

[3]And he answered and said unto them, "I will also ask you one thing; and answer me: [4]The baptism of John, was it from heaven, or of men?"

[5]And they reasoned with themselves, saying, "If we shall say, 'From heaven'; he will say, 'Why then believed ye him

Luke 20

not?' [6]But and if we say, 'Of men'; all the people will stone us: for they be persuaded that John was a prophet."

[7]And they answered, that they could not tell whence it was.

[8]And Jesus said unto them, "Neither tell I you by what authority I do these things."

The Greatest Commandment

Mark 12:28-34

Mark 12

AND ONE OF THE SCRIBES CAME, AND HAVING heard them reasoning together, and perceiving that he had answered them well, asked him, "Which is the first commandment of all?"

[29]And Jesus answered him, "The first of all the commandments is, 'Hear, O Israel; the Lord our God is one Lord: [30]and thou shalt love the Lord thy God with all thy heart, and with all thy soul, and with all thy mind, and with all thy strength': this is the first commandment. [31]And the second is like, namely this, 'Thou shalt love thy neighbour as thyself.' There is none other commandment greater than these."

[32]And the scribe said unto him, "Well, Master, thou hast said the truth: for there is one God; and there is none other but he: [33]and to love him with all the heart, and with all the understanding, and with all the soul, and with all the strength, and to love his neighbour as himself, is more than all whole burnt offerings and sacrifices."

[34]And when Jesus saw that he answered discreetly, he said unto him, "Thou art not far from the kingdom of God." And no man after that durst ask him any question.

The Widow's Mites

Mark 12:41-44

Mark 12

And Jesus sat over against the treasury, and beheld how the people cast money into the treasury: and many that were rich cast in much. [42]And there came a certain poor widow, and she threw in two mites, which make a farthing.

[43]And he called unto him his disciples, and saith unto them, "Verily I say unto you, that this poor widow hath cast more in, than all they which have cast into the treasury: [44]for all they did cast in of their abundance; but she of her want did cast in all that she had, even all her living."

Signs of the End of the World

Matthew 24:1-14

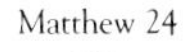

Matthew 24

And Jesus went out, and departed from the temple: and his disciples came to him for to shew him the buildings of the temple. [2]And Jesus said unto them, "See ye not all these things? Verily I say unto you, there shall not be left here one stone upon another, that shall not be thrown down."

[3]And as he sat upon the mount of Olives, the disciples came unto him privately, saying, "Tell us, when shall these things be? And what shall be the sign of thy coming, and of the end of the world?"

[4]And Jesus answered and said unto them, "Take heed that no man deceive you. [5]For many shall come in my name, saying, 'I am Christ'; and shall deceive many. [6]And ye shall hear of wars and rumours of wars: see that ye be not troubled: for all these things must come to pass, but the end is not yet. [7]For nation shall rise against nation, and king

Matthew 24

dom against kingdom: and there shall be famines, and pestilences, and earthquakes, in divers places. [8]All these are the beginning of sorrows.

[9]"Then shall they deliver you up to be afflicted, and shall kill you: and ye shall be hated of all nations for my name's sake. [10]And then shall many be offended, and shall betray one another, and shall hate one another. [11]And many false prophets shall rise, and shall deceive many. [12]And because iniquity shall abound, the love of many shall wax cold. [13]But he that shall endure unto the end, the same shall be saved. [14]And this gospel of the kingdom shall be preached in all the world for a witness unto all nations; and then shall the end come."

The Parable of the Ten Virgins

Matthew 25:1-13

Matthew 25

"THEN SHALL THE KINGDOM OF HEAVEN BE likened unto ten virgins, which took their lamps, and went forth to meet the bridegroom. [2]And five of them were wise, and five were foolish. [3]They that were foolish took their lamps, and took no oil with them: [4]but the wise

The Wise and Foolish Virgins *by Frans Francken the Younger*

took oil in their vessels with their lamps. [5]While the bridegroom tarried, they all slumbered and slept.

[6]"And at midnight there was a cry made, 'Behold, the bridegroom cometh; go ye out to meet him.'

[7]"Then all those virgins arose, and trimmed their lamps. [8]And the foolish said unto the wise, 'Give us of your oil; for our lamps are gone out.'

[9]"But the wise answered, saying, 'Not so; lest there be not enough for us and you: but go ye rather to them that sell, and buy for yourselves.'

[10]"And while they went to buy, the bridegroom came; and they that were ready went in with him to the marriage: and the door was shut.

[11]"Afterward came also the other virgins, saying, 'Lord, Lord, open to us.'

[12]"But he answered and said, 'Verily I say unto you, I know you not.'

[13]"Watch therefore, for ye know neither the day nor the hour wherein the Son of man cometh."

The Parable of the Talents

Matthew 25:14-30

"FOR THE KINGDOM OF HEAVEN IS AS A MAN travelling into a far country, who called his own servants, and delivered unto them his goods. [15]And unto one he gave five talents, to another two, and to another one; to every man according to his several ability; and straightway took his journey. [16]Then he that had received the five talents went and traded with the same, and made them other five talents. [17]And likewise he that had received two, he also gained other two. [18]But he that had received one went and digged in the earth, and hid his lord's money.

[19]"After a long time the lord of those servants cometh, and reckoneth with them. [20]And so he that had received five talents came and brought other five talents, saying,

'Lord, thou deliveredst unto me five talents: behold, I have gained beside them five talents more.'

[21]"His lord said unto him, 'Well done, thou good and faithful servant: thou hast been faithful over a few things, I will make thee ruler over many things: enter thou into the joy of thy lord.'

[22]"He also that had received two talents came and said, 'Lord, thou deliveredst unto me two talents: behold, I have gained two other talents beside them.'

[23]"His lord said unto him, 'Well done, good and faithful servant; thou hast been faithful over a few things, I will make thee ruler over many things: enter thou into the joy of thy lord.'

[24]"Then he which had received the one talent came and said, 'Lord, I knew thee that thou art an hard man, reaping where thou hast not sown, and gathering where thou hast not strawed: [25]and I was afraid, and went and hid thy talent in the earth: lo, there thou hast that is thine.'

[26]"His lord answered and said unto him, 'Thou wicked and slothful servant, thou knewest that I reap where I sowed not, and gather where I have not strawed: [27]thou oughtest therefore to have put my money to the exchangers, and then at my coming I should have received mine own with usury.

[28]" 'Take therefore the talent from him, and give it unto him which hath ten talents. [29]For unto every one that hath shall be given, and he shall have abundance: but from him that hath not shall be taken away even that which he hath. [30]And cast ye the unprofitable servant into outer darkness: there shall be weeping and gnashing of teeth.' "

The Sheep and the Goats

Matthew 25:31-46

Matthew 25

"When the Son of Man shall come in his glory, and all the holy angels with him, then shall he sit upon the throne of his glory: [32]and before him shall be gathered all nations: and he shall separate them one from another, as a shepherd divideth his sheep from the goats: [33]and he shall set the sheep on his right hand, but the goats on the left.

[34]"Then shall the King say unto them on his right hand, 'Come, ye blessed of my Father, inherit the kingdom prepared for you from the foundation of the world: [35]for I was an hungred, and ye gave me meat: I was thirsty, and ye gave me drink: I was a stranger, and ye took me in: [36]naked, and ye clothed me: I was sick, and ye visited me: I was in prison, and ye came unto me.'

[37]"Then shall the righteous answer him, saying, 'Lord, when saw we thee an hungred, and fed thee? Or thirsty, and gave thee drink? [38]When saw we thee a stranger, and took thee in? Or naked, and clothed thee? [39]Or when saw we thee sick, or in prison, and came unto thee?'

[40]"And the King shall answer and say unto them, 'Verily I say unto you, inasmuch as ye have done it unto one of the least of these my brethren, ye have done it unto me.'

[41]"Then shall he say also unto them on the left hand, 'Depart from me, ye cursed, into everlasting fire, prepared for the devil and his angels: [42]for I was an hungred, and ye gave me no meat: I was thirsty, and ye gave me no drink: [43]I was a stranger, and ye took me not in: naked, and ye clothed me not: sick, or in prison, and ye visited me not.'

[44]"Then shall they also answer him, saying, 'Lord, when saw we thee an hungred, or athirst, or a stranger, or naked, or sick, or in prison, and did not minister unto thee?'

[45]"Then shall he answer them, saying, 'Verily I say unto you, inasmuch as ye did it not to one of the least of these, ye did it not to me.'

[46]"And these shall go away into everlasting punishment: but the righteous into life eternal."

Luke 22

JUDAS RECEIVES THIRTY PIECES OF SILVER *by Duccio di Buoninsegna*

JUDAS AGREES TO BETRAY JESUS

LUKE 22:1-6

Luke 22

NOW THE FEAST OF UNLEAVENED BREAD DREW nigh, which is called the Passover. [2]And the chief priests and scribes sought how they might kill him; for they feared the people. [3]Then entered Satan into Judas surnamed Iscariot, being of the number of the twelve. [4]And he went his way, and communed with the chief priests and captains, how he might betray him unto them. [5]And they were glad, and covenanted to give him money. [6]And he promised, and sought opportunity to betray him unto them in the absence of the multitude.

The Last Supper

Luke 22:7-20

Luke 22

THEN CAME THE DAY OF UNLEAVENED BREAD, when the passover must be killed. [8]And he sent Peter and John, saying, "Go and prepare us the passover, that we may eat."

[9]And they said unto him, "Where wilt thou that we prepare?"

[10]And he said unto them, "Behold, when ye are entered into the city, there shall a man meet you, bearing a pitcher of water; follow him into the house where he entereth in. [11]And ye shall say unto the goodman of the house, 'The Master saith unto thee, "Where is the guestchamber, where I shall eat the passover with my disciples?"' [12]And he shall shew you a large upper room furnished: there make ready."

[13]And they went, and found as he had said unto them: and they made ready the passover.

[14]And when the hour was come, he sat down, and the twelve apostles with him. [15]And he said unto them, "With desire I have desired to eat this passover with you before I

THE LAST SUPPER *by Vincente Masip*

Luke 22

suffer: [16]for I say unto you, I will not any more eat thereof, until it be fulfilled in the kingdom of God."

[17]And he took the cup, and gave thanks, and said, "Take this, and divide it among yourselves: [18]for I say unto you, I will not drink of the fruit of the vine, until the kingdom of God shall come."

[19]And he took bread, and gave thanks, and brake it, and gave unto them, saying, "This is my body which is given for you: this do in remembrance of me."

[20]Likewise also the cup after supper, saying, "This cup is the new testament in my blood, which is shed for you."

Jesus Washes His Disciples' Feet

John 13:2-30

John 13

And supper being ended, the devil having now put into the heart of Judas Iscariot, Simon's son, to betray him; [3]Jesus knowing that the Father had given all things into his hands, and that he was come from God, and went to God; [4]he riseth from supper, and laid aside his garments; and took a towel, and girded himself. [5]After that he poureth water into a basin, and began to wash the disciples' feet, and to wipe them with the towel wherewith he was girded.

[6]Then cometh he to Simon Peter: and Peter saith unto him, "Lord, dost thou wash my feet?"

[7]Jesus answered and said unto him, "What I do thou knowest not now; but thou shalt know hereafter."

[8]Peter saith unto him, "Thou shalt never wash my feet."

Jesus answered him, "If I wash thee not, thou hast no part with me."

[9]Simon Peter saith unto him, "Lord, not my feet only, but also my hands and my head."

[10]Jesus saith to him, "He that is washed needeth not save to wash his feet, but is clean every whit: and ye are clean, but not all." [11]For he knew who should betray him; therefore said he, "Ye are not all clean."

John 13

CHRIST WASHING THE DISCIPLES' FEET *by Duccio di Buoninsegna*

John 13

[12]So after he had washed their feet, and had taken his garments, and was set down again, he said unto them, "Know ye what I have done to you? [13]Ye call me Master and Lord: and ye say well; for so I am. [14]If I then, your Lord and Master, have washed your feet; ye also ought to wash one another's feet. [15]For I have given you an example, that ye should do as I have done to you. [16]Verily, verily, I say unto you, the servant is not greater than his lord; neither he that is sent greater than he that sent him. [17]If ye know these things, happy are ye if ye do them.

[18]"I speak not of you all: I know whom I have chosen: but that the scripture may be fulfilled, 'He that eateth bread with me hath lifted up his heel against me.'

[19]"Now I tell you before it come, that, when it is come to pass, ye may believe that I am he. [20]Verily, verily, I say unto you, he that receiveth whomsoever I send receiveth me; and he that receiveth me receiveth him that sent me."

[21]When Jesus had thus said, he was troubled in spirit, and testified, and said, "Verily, verily, I say unto you, that one of you shall betray me."

John 13

[22]Then the disciples looked one on another, doubting of whom he spake. [23]Now there was leaning on Jesus' bosom one of his disciples, whom Jesus loved. [24]Simon Peter therefore beckoned to him, that he should ask who it should be of whom he spake.

[25]He then lying on Jesus' breast saith unto him, "Lord, who is it?"

[26]Jesus answered, "He it is, to whom I shall give a sop, when I have dipped it." And when he had dipped the sop, he gave it to Judas Iscariot, the son of Simon. [27]And after the sop Satan entered into him.

Then said Jesus unto him, "That thou doest, do quickly." [28]Now no man at the table knew for what intent he spake this unto him. [29]For some of them thought, because Judas had the bag, that Jesus had said unto him, "Buy those things that we have need of against the feast"; or, that he should give something to the poor. [30]He then having received the sop went immediately out: and it was night.

A New Commandment

John 13:31-38

John 13

Therefore, when he was gone out, Jesus said, "Now is the Son of man glorified, and God is glorified in him. [32]If God be glorified in him, God shall also glorify him in himself, and shall straightway glorify him.

[33]"Little children, yet a little while I am with you. Ye shall seek me: and as I said unto the Jews, 'Whither I go, ye cannot come'; so now I say to you.

[34]"A new commandment I give unto you, that ye love one another; as I have loved you, that ye also love one another. [35]By this shall all men know that ye are my disciples, if ye have love one to another."

[36]Simon Peter said unto him, "Lord, whither goest thou?"

Jesus answered him, "Whither I go, thou canst not follow me now; but thou shalt follow me afterwards."

John 13

[37]Peter said unto him, "Lord, why cannot I follow thee now? I will lay down my life for thy sake."

[38]Jesus answered him, "Wilt thou lay down thy life for my sake? Verily, verily, I say unto thee, the cock shall not crow, till thou hast denied me thrice."

The Way, the Truth, and the Life

John 14

"LET NOT YOUR HEART BE TROUBLED: YE BELIEVE in God, believe also in me. [2]In my Father's house are many mansions: if it were not so, I would have told you. I go to prepare a place for you. [3]And if I go and prepare a place for you, I will come again, and receive you unto myself; that where I am, there ye may be also. [4]And whither I go ye know, and the way ye know."

John 14

[5]Thomas saith unto him, "Lord, we know not whither thou goest; and how can we know the way?"

[6]Jesus saith unto him, "I am the way, the truth, and the life: no man cometh unto the Father, but by me. [7]If ye had known me, ye should have known my Father also: and from henceforth ye know him, and have seen him."

[8]Philip saith unto him, "Lord, shew us the Father, and it sufficeth us."

[9]Jesus saith unto him, "Have I been so long time with you, and yet hast thou not known me, Philip? He that hath seen me hath seen the Father; and how sayest thou then, 'Shew us the Father'? [10]Believest thou not that I am in the Father, and the Father in me? The words that I speak unto you I speak not of myself: but the Father that dwelleth in me, he doeth the works. [11]Believe me that I am in the Father, and the Father in me: or else believe me for the very works' sake. [12]Verily, verily, I say unto you, he that believeth on me, the works that I do shall he do also; and greater works than these shall he do; because I go unto my Father.

John 14

[13]And whatsoever ye shall ask in my name, that will I do, that the Father may be glorified in the Son. [14]If ye shall ask any thing in my name, I will do it.

[15]"If ye love me, keep my commandments. [16]And I will pray the Father, and he shall give you another Comforter, that he may abide with you for ever; [17]even the Spirit of truth; whom the world cannot receive, because it seeth him not, neither knoweth him: but ye know him; for he dwelleth with you, and shall be in you. [18]I will not leave you comfortless: I will come to you. [19]Yet a little while, and the world seeth me no more; but ye see me: because I live, ye shall live also. [20]At that day ye shall know that I am in my Father, and ye in me, and I in you. [21]He that hath my commandments, and keepeth them, he it is that loveth me: and he that loveth me shall be loved of my Father, and I will love him, and will manifest myself to him."

[22]Judas saith unto him, not Iscariot, "Lord, how is it that thou wilt manifest thyself unto us, and not unto the world?"

[23]Jesus answered and said unto him, "If a man love me, he will keep my words: and my Father will love him, and we will come unto him, and make our abode with him. [24]He that loveth me not keepeth not my sayings: and the word which ye hear is not mine, but the Father's which sent me.

[25]"These things have I spoken unto you, being yet present with you. [26]But the Comforter, which is the Holy Ghost, whom the Father will send in my name, he shall teach you all things, and bring all things to your remembrance, whatsoever I have said unto you. [27]Peace I leave with you, my peace I give unto you: not as the world giveth, give I unto you. Let not your heart be troubled, neither let it be afraid.

[28]"Ye have heard how I said unto you, 'I go away, and come again unto you.' If ye loved me, ye would rejoice, because I said, 'I go unto the Father': for my Father is greater than I. [29]And now I have told you before it come to pass, that, when it is come to pass, ye might believe. [30]Hereafter I will not talk much with you: for the prince of this world cometh, and hath nothing in me. [31]But that the world may know that I love the Father; and as the Father gave me commandment, even so I do.

"Arise, let us go hence."

The True Vine

John 15:1-17

John 15

"I am the true vine, and my Father is the husbandman. [2]Every branch in me that beareth not fruit he taketh away: and every branch that beareth fruit, he purgeth it, that it may bring forth more fruit. [3]Now ye are clean through the word which I have spoken unto you. [4]Abide in me, and I in you. As the branch cannot bear fruit of itself, except it abide in the vine; no more can ye, except ye abide in me.

[5]"I am the vine, ye are the branches: he that abideth in me, and I in him, the same bringeth forth much fruit: for without me ye can do nothing.

[6]"If a man abide not in me, he is cast forth as a branch, and is withered; and men gather them, and cast them into the fire, and they are burned. [7]If ye abide in me, and my words abide in you, ye shall ask what ye will, and it shall be done unto you.

[8]"Herein is my Father glorified, that ye bear much fruit; so shall ye be my disciples.

[9]"As the Father hath loved me, so have I loved you: continue ye in my love. [10]If ye keep my commandments, ye shall abide in my love; even as I have kept my Father's commandments, and abide in his love. [11]These things have I spoken unto you, that my joy might remain in you, and that your joy might be full.

[12]"This is my commandment, that ye love one another, as I have loved you. [13]Greater love hath no man than this, that a man lay down his life for his friends. [14]Ye are my friends, if ye do whatsoever I command you. [15]Henceforth I call you not servants; for the servant knoweth not what his lord doeth: but I have called you friends; for all things that I have heard of my Father I have made known unto you.

[16]"Ye have not chosen me, but I have chosen you, and ordained you, that ye should go and bring forth fruit, and that your fruit should remain: that whatsoever ye shall ask of the Father in my name, he may give it you. [17]These things I command you, that ye love one another."

"Ask, and Ye Shall Receive"

John 16:24-33

John 16

"HITHERTO HAVE YE ASKED NOTHING IN MY name: ask, and ye shall receive, that your joy may be full.

[25]"These things have I spoken unto you in proverbs: but the time cometh, when I shall no more speak unto you in proverbs, but I shall shew you plainly of the Father. [26]At that day ye shall ask in my name: and I say not unto you, that I will pray the Father for you: [27]for the Father himself loveth you, because ye have loved me, and have believed that I came out from God. [28]I came forth from the Father, and am come into the world: again, I leave the world, and go to the Father."

[29]His disciples said unto him, "Lo, now speakest thou plainly, and speakest no proverb. [30]Now are we sure that thou knowest all things, and needest not that any man should ask thee: by this we believe that thou camest forth from God."

[31]Jesus answered them, "Do ye now believe? [32]Behold, the hour cometh, yea, is now come, that ye shall be scattered, every man to his own, and shall leave me alone: and yet I am not alone, because the Father is with me.

[33]"These things I have spoken unto you, that in me ye might have peace. In the world ye shall have tribulation: but be of good cheer; I have overcome the world."

Gethsemane

Matthew 26:36-56

Matthew 26

THEN COMETH JESUS WITH THEM UNTO A PLACE called Gethsemane, and saith unto the disciples, "Sit ye here, while I go and pray yonder." [37]And he took with him Peter and the two sons of Zebedee, and began to be sorrowful and very heavy. [38]Then saith he unto them, "My soul is

exceeding sorrowful, even unto death: tarry ye here, and watch with me."

[39]And he went a little farther, and fell on his face, and prayed, saying, "O my Father, if it be possible, let this cup pass from me: nevertheless not as I will, but as thou wilt."

[40]And he cometh unto the disciples, and findeth them asleep, and saith unto Peter, "What, could ye not watch with me one hour? [41]Watch and pray, that ye enter not into

THE AGONY IN THE GARDEN *by Sandro Botticelli*

The Arrest of Jesus *by Fra Angelico*

temptation: the spirit indeed is willing, but the flesh is weak."

[42]He went away again the second time, and prayed, saying, "O my Father, if this cup may not pass away from me, except I drink it, thy will be done."

[43]And he came and found them asleep again: for their eyes were heavy. [44]And he left them, and went away again, and prayed the third time, saying the same words.

[45]Then cometh he to his disciples, and saith unto them, "Sleep on now, and take your rest: behold, the hour is at hand, and the Son of man is betrayed into the hands of sinners. [46]Rise, let us be going: behold, he is at hand that doth betray me."

[47]And while he yet spake, lo, Judas, one of the twelve, came, and with him a great multitude with swords and staves, from the chief priests and elders of the people.

Matthew 26

[48]Now he that betrayed him gave them a sign, saying, "Whomsoever I shall kiss, that same is he: hold him fast." [49]And forthwith he came to Jesus, and said, "Hail, master"; and kissed him.

[50]And Jesus said unto him, "Friend, wherefore art thou come?"

Then came they, and laid hands on Jesus, and took him. [51]And, behold, one of them which were with Jesus stretched out his hand, and drew his sword, and struck a servant of the high priest's, and smote off his ear.

[52]Then said Jesus unto him, "Put up again thy sword into his place: for all they that take the sword shall perish with the sword. [53]Thinkest thou that I cannot now pray to my Father, and he shall presently give me more than twelve legions of angels? [54]But how then shall the scriptures be fulfilled, that thus it must be?"

[55]In that same hour said Jesus to the multitudes, "Are ye come out as against a thief with swords and staves for to take me? I sat daily with you teaching in the temple, and ye laid no hold on me. [56]But all this was done, that the scriptures of the prophets might be fulfilled." Then all the disciples forsook him, and fled.

JESUS BEFORE CAIAPHAS

MATTHEW 26:57-75

Matthew 26

AND THEY THAT HAD LAID HOLD ON JESUS LED HIM away to Caiaphas the high priest, where the scribes and the elders were assembled. [58]But Peter followed him afar off unto the high priest's palace, and went in, and sat with the servants, to see the end.

[59]Now the chief priests, and elders, and all the council, sought false witness against Jesus, to put him to death; [60]but found none: yea, though many false witnesses came, yet found they none.

At the last came two false witnesses, [61]and said, "This fellow said, 'I am able to destroy the temple of God, and to build it in three days.'"

Matthew 26

[62]And the high priest arose, and said unto him, "Answerest thou nothing? What is it which these witness against thee?" [63]But Jesus held his peace.

And the high priest answered and said unto him, "I adjure thee by the living God, that thou tell us whether thou be the Christ, the Son of God."

[64]Jesus saith unto him, "Thou hast said: nevertheless I say unto you, hereafter shall ye see the Son of man sitting on the right hand of power, and coming in the clouds of heaven."

[65]Then the high priest rent his clothes, saying, "He hath spoken blasphemy; what further need have we of witnesses? Behold, now ye have heard his blasphemy. [66]What think ye?"

They answered and said, "He is guilty of death."

[67]Then did they spit in his face, and buffeted him; and others smote him with the palms of their hands, [68]saying,

CHRIST BEFORE CAIAPHAS *by Ambrogio Bondone Giotto*

Matthew 26

"Prophesy unto us, thou Christ, who is he that smote thee?"

[69]Now Peter sat without in the palace: and a damsel came unto him, saying, "Thou also wast with Jesus of Galilee."

[70]But he denied before them all, saying, "I know not what thou sayest."

[71]And when he was gone out into the porch, another maid saw him, and said unto them that were there, "This fellow was also with Jesus of Nazareth."

[72]And again he denied with an oath, "I do not know the man."

[73]And after a while came unto him they that stood by, and said to Peter, "Surely thou also art one of them; for thy speech bewrayeth thee."

[74]Then began he to curse and to swear, saying, "I know not the man."

And immediately the cock crew. [75]And Peter remembered the word of Jesus, which said unto him, "Before the cock crow, thou shalt deny me thrice." And he went out, and wept bitterly.

Judas Hangs Himself

Matthew 27:1-10

Matthew 27

When the morning was come, all the chief priests and elders of the people took counsel against Jesus to put him to death: [2]and when they had bound him, they led him away, and delivered him to Pontius Pilate the governor.

[3]Then Judas, which had betrayed him, when he saw that he was condemned, repented himself, and brought again the thirty pieces of silver to the chief priests and elders, [4]saying, "I have sinned in that I have betrayed the innocent blood."

And they said, "What is that to us? See thou to that."

[5]And he cast down the pieces of silver in the temple, and departed, and went and hanged himself.

Matthew 27

[6]And the chief priests took the silver pieces, and said, "It is not lawful for to put them into the treasury, because it is the price of blood." [7]And they took counsel, and bought with them the potter's field, to bury strangers in. [8]Wherefore that field was called, "The field of blood", unto this day. [9]Then was fulfilled that which was spoken by Jeremy the prophet, saying, "And they took the thirty pieces of silver, the price of him that was valued, whom they of the children of Israel did value; [10]and gave them for the potter's field, as the Lord appointed me."

Jesus Before Pilate

John 18:28-19:16

John 18

THEN LED THEY JESUS FROM CAIAPHAS UNTO THE hall of judgment: and it was early; and they themselves went not into the judgment hall, lest they should be defiled; but that they might eat the passover. [29]Pilate then went out unto them, and said, "What accusation bring ye against this man?"

[30]They answered and said unto him, "If he were not a malefactor, we would not have delivered him up unto thee."

[31]Then said Pilate unto them, "Take ye him, and judge him according to your law."

The Jews therefore said unto him, "It is not lawful for us to put any man to death": [32]that the saying of Jesus might be fulfilled, which he spake, signifying what death he should die.

[33]Then Pilate entered into the judgment hall again, and called Jesus, and said unto him, "Art thou the King of the Jews?"

[34]Jesus answered him, "Sayest thou this thing of thyself, or did others tell it thee of me?"

[35]Pilate answered, "Am I a Jew? Thine own nation and the chief priests have delivered thee unto me: what hast thou done?"

John 18

[36]Jesus answered, "My kingdom is not of this world: if my kingdom were of this world, then would my servants fight, that I should not be delivered to the Jews: but now is my kingdom not from hence."

[37]Pilate therefore said unto him, "Art thou a king then?"

Jesus answered, "Thou sayest that I am a king. To this end was I born, and for this cause came I into the world, that I should bear witness unto the truth. Every one that is of the truth heareth my voice."

[38]Pilate saith unto him, "What is truth?" And when he had said this, he went out again unto the Jews, and saith unto them, "I find in him no fault at all. [30]But ye have a custom, that I should release unto you one at the passover: will ye therefore that I release unto you the King of the Jews?"

[40]Then cried they all again, saying, "Not this man, but Barabbas." Now Barabbas was a robber.

John 19

THEN PILATE THEREFORE TOOK JESUS, AND SCOURGED HIM. [2]And the soldiers plaited a crown of thorns, and put it on his head, and they put on him a purple robe, [3]and said, "Hail, King of the Jews!" And they smote him with their hands.

[4]Pilate therefore went forth again, and saith unto them, "Behold, I bring him forth to you, that ye may know that I find no fault in him." [5]Then came Jesus forth, wearing the crown of thorns, and the purple robe. And Pilate saith unto them, "Behold the man!"

[6]When the chief priests therefore and officers saw him, they cried out, saying, "Crucify him, crucify him."

Pilate saith unto them, "Take ye him, and crucify him: for I find no fault in him."

[7]The Jews answered him, "We have a law, and by our law he ought to die, because he made himself the Son of God."

[8]When Pilate therefore heard that saying, he was the more afraid; [9]and went again into the judgment hall, and saith unto Jesus, "Whence art thou?" But Jesus gave him no

'Ecce Homo!' *by Quentin Massys*

answer. [10]Then saith Pilate unto him, "Speakest thou not unto me? Knowest thou not that I have power to crucify thee, and have power to release thee?"

[11]Jesus answered, "Thou couldest have no power at all against me, except it were given thee from above: therefore he that delivered me unto thee hath the greater sin."

[12]And from thenceforth Pilate sought to release him: but the Jews cried out, saying, "If thou let this man go, thou art not Caesar's friend: whosoever maketh himself a king speaketh against Caesar."

John 19

[13]When Pilate therefore heard that saying, he brought Jesus forth, and sat down in the judgment seat in a place that is called the Pavement, but in the Hebrew, Gabbatha. [14]And it was the preparation of the passover, and about the sixth hour: and he saith unto the Jews, "Behold your King!"

[15]But they cried out, "Away with him, away with him, crucify him."

Pilate saith unto them, "Shall I crucify your King?"

The chief priests answered, "We have no king but Caesar."

[16]Then delivered he him therefore unto them to be crucified. And they took Jesus, and led him away.

The Crucifixion

Luke 23:26-47

Luke 23

And as they led him away, they laid hold upon one Simon, a Cyrenian, coming out of the country, and on him they laid the cross, that he might bear it after Jesus. [27]And there followed him a great company of people, and of women, which also bewailed and lamented him. [28]But Jesus turning unto them said, "Daughters of Jerusalem, weep not for me, but weep for yourselves, and for your children. [29]For, behold, the days are coming, in the which they shall say, 'Blessed are the barren, and the wombs that never bare, and the paps which never gave suck.' [30]Then shall they begin to say to the mountains, 'Fall on us'; and to the hills, 'Cover us.' [31]For if they do these things in a green tree, what shall be done in the dry?"

[32]And there were also two other, malefactors, led with him to be put to death. [33]And when they were come to the place, which is called Calvary, there they crucified him, and the malefactors, one on the right hand, and the other on the left. [34]Then said Jesus, "Father, forgive them; for they know not what they do." And they parted his raiment, and cast lots.

Luke 23

CHRIST FALLS ON THE WAY TO CALVARY *by Raphael*

Luke 23

[35]And the people stood beholding. And the rulers also with them derided him, saying, "He saved others; let him save himself, if he be Christ, the chosen of God."

[36]And the soldiers also mocked him, coming to him, and offering him vinegar, [37]and saying, "If thou be the king of the Jews, save thyself."

[38]And a superscription also was written over him in letters of Greek, and Latin, and Hebrew, THIS IS THE KING OF THE JEWS.

The Crucifixion *by Pietro Perugino*

Luke 23

[39]And one of the malefactors which were hanged railed on him, saying, "If thou be Christ, save thyself and us."

[40]But the other answering rebuked him, saying, "Dost not thou fear God, seeing thou art in the same condemnation? [41]And we indeed justly; for we receive the due reward of our deeds: but this man hath done nothing amiss."

[42]And he said unto Jesus, "Lord, remember me when thou comest into thy kingdom."

[43]And Jesus said unto him, "Verily I say unto thee, to day shalt thou be with me in paradise."

[44]And it was about the sixth hour, and there was a darkness over all the earth until the ninth hour. [45]And the sun was darkened, and the veil of the temple was rent in the midst. [46]And when Jesus had cried with a loud voice, he said, "Father, into thy hands I commend my spirit": and having said thus, he gave up the ghost.

[47]Now when the centurion saw what was done, he glorified God, saying, "Certainly this was a righteous man."

Jesus Laid in the Tomb

Matthew 27:55-66

Matthew 27

AND MANY WOMEN WERE THERE BEHOLDING AFAR off, which followed Jesus from Galilee, ministering unto him: [56]among which was Mary Magdalene, and Mary the mother of James and Joses, and the mother of Zebedee's children.

[57]When the even was come, there came a rich man of Arimathaea, named Joseph, who also himself was Jesus' disciple: [58]he went to Pilate, and begged the body of Jesus. Then Pilate commanded the body to be delivered. [59]And when Joseph had taken the body, he wrapped it in a clean linen cloth, [60]and laid it in his own new tomb, which he had hewn out in the rock: and he rolled a great stone to the door of the sepulchre, and departed. [61]And there was Mary Magdalene, and the other Mary, sitting over against the sepulchre.

THE DEPOSITION OF CHRIST *by Filippino Lippi and Pietro Perugino*

[62]Now the next day, that followed the day of the preparation, the chief priests and Pharisees came together unto Pilate, [63]saying, "Sir, we remember that that deceiver said, while he was yet alive, 'After three days I will rise again.' [64]Command therefore that the sepulchre be made sure until the third day, lest his disciples come by night,

Matthew 27

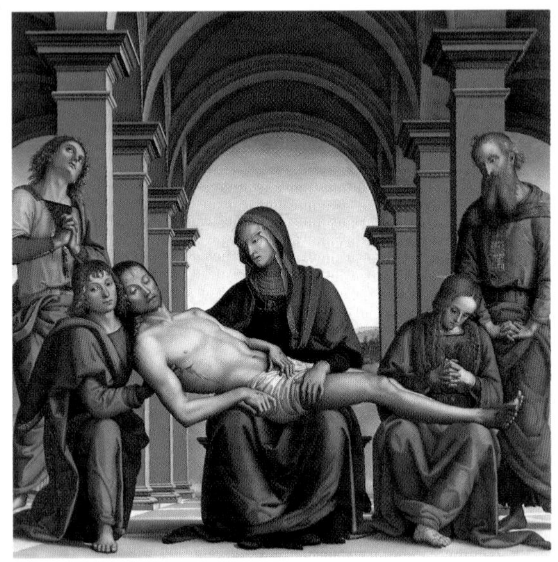

PIETA, THE DEAD CHRIST *by Pietro Perugino*

Matthew 27

and steal him away, and say unto the people, 'He is risen from the dead': so the last error shall be worse than the first."

[65]Pilate said unto them, "Ye have a watch: go your way, make it as sure as ye can." [66]So they went, and made the sepulchre sure, sealing the stone, and setting a watch.

The Resurrection

John 20:1-18

John 20

THE FIRST DAY OF THE WEEK COMETH MARY Magdalene early, when it was yet dark, unto the sepulchre, and seeth the stone taken away from the sepulchre. [2]Then she runneth, and cometh to Simon Peter, and to the other disciple, whom Jesus loved, and saith unto them, "They have taken away the Lord out of the sepulchre, and we know not where they have laid him." [3]Peter therefore went forth, and that other disciple, and came to the sepulchre. [4]So they ran both together: and the other disciple did outrun Peter, and came first to the sepulchre. [5]And he stooping down, and looking in, saw the linen clothes lying; yet went he not in. [6]Then cometh Simon Peter following him, and went into the sepulchre, and seeth the linen clothes lie, [7]and the napkin, that was about his head, not lying with the linen clothes, but wrapped together in a place by itself. [8]Then went in also that other disciple, which came first to the sepulchre, and he saw, and believed. [9]For as yet they knew not the scripture, that he must rise again from the dead.

[10]Then the disciples went away again unto their own home. [11]But Mary stood without at the sepulchre weeping: and as she wept, she stooped down, and looked into the sepulchre, [12]and seeth two angels in white sitting, the one at the head, and the other at the feet, where the body of Jesus had lain.

[13]And they say unto her, "Woman, why weepest thou?"

She saith unto them, "Because they have taken away my Lord, and I know not where they have laid him." [14]And when she had thus said, she turned herself back, and saw Jesus standing, and knew not that it was Jesus.

[15]Jesus saith unto her, "Woman, why weepest thou? Whom seekest thou?"

She, supposing him to be the gardener, saith unto him, "Sir, if thou have borne him hence, tell me where thou hast laid him, and I will take him away."

[16]Jesus saith unto her, "Mary."

CHRIST RISING FROM HIS TOMB *by Fra Angelico*

She turned herself, and saith unto him, "Rabboni"; which is to say, Master.

[17]Jesus saith unto her, "Touch me not; for I am not yet ascended to my Father: but go to my brethren, and say unto them, 'I ascend unto my Father, and your Father; and to my God, and your God.'"

[18]Mary Magdalene came and told the disciples that she had seen the Lord, and that he had spoken these things unto her.

The Walk to Emmaus

Luke 24:13-36

Luke 24

AND, BEHOLD, TWO OF THEM WENT THAT SAME day to a village called Emmaus, which was from Jerusalem about threescore furlongs. [14]And they talked together of all these things which had happened. [15]And it came to pass, that, while they communed together and reasoned, Jesus himself drew near, and went with them. [16]But their eyes were holden that they should not know him.

[17]And he said unto them, "What manner of communications are these that ye have one to another, as ye walk, and are sad?"

[18]And the one of them, whose name was Cleopas, answering said unto him, "Art thou only a stranger in Jerusalem, and hast not known the things which are come to pass there in these days?"

[19]And he said unto them, "What things?"

And they said unto him, "Concerning Jesus of Nazareth, which was a prophet mighty in deed and word before God and all the people: [20]and how the chief priests and our rulers delivered him to be condemned to death, and have crucified him.

[21]"But we trusted that it had been he which should have redeemed Israel: and beside all this, to day is the third day since these things were done.

[22]"Yea, and certain women also of our company made us astonished, which were early at the sepulchre; [23]and when they found not his body, they came, saying, that they had also seen a vision of angels, which said that he was alive. [24]And certain of them which were with us went to the sepulchre, and found it even so as the women had said: but him they saw not."

[25]Then he said unto them, "O fools, and slow of heart to believe all that the prophets have spoken: [26]ought not Christ to have suffered these things, and to enter into his glory?" [27]And beginning at Moses and all the prophets, he expounded unto them in all the scriptures the things concerning himself.

Luke 24

[28]And they drew nigh unto the village, whither they went: and he made as though he would have gone further. [29]But they constrained him, saying, "Abide with us: for it is toward evening, and the day is far spent." And he went in to tarry with them.

[30]And it came to pass, as he sat at meat with them, he took bread, and blessed it, and brake, and gave to them. [31]And their eyes were opened, and they knew him; and he vanished out of their sight. [32]And they said one to another, "Did not our heart burn within us, while he talked with us by the way, and while he opened to us the scriptures?"

[33]And they rose up the same hour, and returned to Jerusalem, and found the eleven gathered together, and them that were with them, [34]saying, "The Lord is risen indeed, and hath appeared to Simon." [35]And they told what things were done in the way, and how he was known of them in breaking of bread.

[36]And as they thus spake, Jesus himself stood in the midst of them, and saith unto them, "Peace be unto you."

Doubting Thomas

John 20:20-31

John 20

AND WHEN HE HAD SO SAID, HE SHEWED UNTO them his hands and his side. Then were the disciples glad, when they saw the Lord.

[21]Then said Jesus to them again, "Peace be unto you: as my Father hath sent me, even so send I you." [22]And when he had said this, he breathed on them, and saith unto them, "Receive ye the Holy Ghost: [23]whose soever sins ye remit, they are remitted unto them, and whose soever sins ye retain, they are retained."

[24]But Thomas, one of the twelve, called Didymus, was not with them when Jesus came. [25]The other disciples therefore said unto him, "We have seen the Lord."

But he said unto them, "Except I shall see in his hands the print of the nails, and put my finger into the print of the nails, and thrust my hand into his side, I will not believe."

CHRIST ON THE ROAD TO EMMAUS *by Jacques de Stella*

[26]And after eight days again his disciples were within, and Thomas with them: then came Jesus, the doors being shut, and stood in the midst, and said, "Peace be unto you." [27]Then saith he to Thomas, "Reach hither thy finger, and behold my hands; and reach hither thy hand,

John 20

and thrust it into my side: and be not faithless, but believing."

[28] And Thomas answered and said unto him, "My Lord and my God."

[29] Jesus saith unto him, "Thomas, because thou hast seen me, thou hast believed: blessed are they that have not seen, and yet have believed."

DOUBTING THOMAS *by Caravaggio*

John 20

[30] And many other signs truly did Jesus in the presence of his disciples, which are not written in this book: [31] but these are written, that ye might believe that Jesus is the Christ, the Son of God; and that believing ye might have life through his name.

Peter's Reinstatement

John 21:1-19

John 21

After these things Jesus shewed himself again to the disciples at the sea of Tiberias; and on this wise shewed he himself. [2]There were together Simon Peter, and Thomas called Didymus, and Nathanael of Cana in Galilee, and the sons of Zebedee, and two other of his disciples. [3]Simon Peter saith unto them, "I go a fishing." They say unto him, "We also go with thee." They went forth, and entered into a ship immediately, and that night they caught nothing.

[4]But when the morning was now come, Jesus stood on the shore: but the disciples knew not that it was Jesus.

[5]Then Jesus saith unto them, "Children, have ye any meat?"

They answered him, "No."

[6]And he said unto them, "Cast the net on the right side of the ship, and ye shall find." They cast therefore, and now they were not able to draw it for the multitude of fishes.

[7]Therefore that disciple whom Jesus loved saith unto Peter, "It is the Lord." Now when Simon Peter heard that it was the Lord, he girt his fisher's coat unto him, (for he was naked,) and did cast himself into the sea. [8]And the other disciples came in a little ship; (for they were not far from land, but as it were two hundred cubits,) dragging the net with fishes. [9]As soon then as they were come to land, they saw a fire of coals there, and fish laid thereon, and bread.

[10]Jesus saith unto them, "Bring of the fish which ye have now caught."

[11]Simon Peter went up, and drew the net to land full of great fishes, an hundred and fifty and three: and for all there were so many, yet was not the net broken. [12]Jesus saith unto them, "Come and dine." And none of the disciples durst ask him, "Who art thou?" knowing that it was the Lord. [13]Jesus then cometh, and taketh bread, and giveth them, and fish likewise. [14]This is now the third time

John 21

CHRIST'S CHARGE TO ST PETER *by Raphael*

John 21

that Jesus shewed himself to his disciples, after that he was risen from the dead.

[15]So when they had dined, Jesus saith to Simon Peter, "Simon, son of Jonas, lovest thou me more than these?"

He saith unto him, "Yea, Lord; thou knowest that I love thee."

He saith unto him, "Feed my lambs."

[16]He saith to him again the second time, "Simon, son of Jonas, lovest thou me?"

He saith unto him, "Yea, Lord; thou knowest that I love thee."

He saith unto him, "Feed my sheep."

[17]He saith unto him the third time, "Simon, son of Jonas, lovest thou me?"

Peter was grieved because he said unto him the third time, "Lovest thou me?" And he said unto him, "Lord, thou knowest all things; thou knowest that I love thee."

Jesus saith unto him, "Feed my sheep. [18]Verily, verily, I say unto thee, when thou wast young, thou girdedst thyself, and walkedst whither thou wouldest: but when thou shalt be old, thou shalt stretch forth thy hands, and another shall gird thee, and carry thee whither thou wouldest not." [19]This spake he, signifying by what death he should glorify God. And when he had spoken this, he saith unto him, "Follow me."

John 21

THE GREAT COMMISSION

MATTHEW 28: 16-20

Matthew 28

THEN THE ELEVEN DISCIPLES WENT AWAY INTO Galilee, into a mountain where Jesus had appointed them. [17]And when they saw him, they worshipped him: but some doubted. [18]And Jesus came and spake unto them, saying, "All power is given unto me in heaven and in earth. [19]Go ye therefore, and teach all nations, baptizing them in the name of the Father, and of the Son, and of the Holy Ghost: [20]teaching them to observe all things whatsoever I have commanded you: and, lo, I am with you alway, even unto the end of the world." Amen.

THE ORDINATION by Nicolas Poussin

St Peter Visited in Jail by St Paul *by Filippino Lippi*

Chapter & Verses
FROM

THE ACTS *OF THE* APOSTLES

THE ASCENSION • THE DAY OF PENTECOST • THE HEALING AT THE BEAUTIFUL GATE • ANANIAS AND SAPPHIRA • THE CHOOSING OF THE SEVEN • THE MARTYRDOM OF STEPHEN • PHILIP AND THE ETHIOPIAN EUNUCH • THE CONVERSION OF SAUL • PETER AND CORNELIUS • THE CHURCH IN ANTIOCH • PETER DELIVERED BY AN ANGEL • THE DEATH OF HEROD • PAUL AND BARNABAS AT LYSTRA • PAUL'S VISION OF THE MAN OF MACEDONIA • PAUL ARRESTED • BEFORE THE SANHEDRIN • THE PLOT TO KILL PAUL • BEFORE FELIX AND FESTUS • PAUL'S VOYAGE AND SHIPWRECK • PAUL IN ROME

The Ascension

Chapter 1

THE FORMER TREATISE HAVE I MADE, O THEOPHI-lus, of all that Jesus began both to do and teach, [2]until the day in which he was taken up, after that he through the Holy Ghost had given commandments unto the apostles whom he had chosen: [3]to whom also he shewed himself alive after his passion by many infallible proofs, being seen of them forty days, and speaking of the things pertaining to the kingdom of God: [4]and, being assembled together with them, commanded them that they should not depart from Jerusalem, but wait for the promise of the Father, "which", saith he, "ye have heard of me. [5]For John truly baptized with water: but ye shall be baptized with the Holy Ghost not many days hence."

[6]When they therefore were come together, they asked of him, saying, "Lord, wilt thou at this time restore again the kingdom to Israel?"

[7]And he said unto them, "It is not for you to know the times or the seasons, which the Father hath put in his own power. [8]But ye shall receive power, after that the Holy Ghost is come upon you: and ye shall be witnesses unto me both in Jerusalem, and in all Judaea, and in Samaria, and unto the uttermost part of the earth."

[9]And when he had spoken these things, while they beheld, he was taken up; and a cloud received him out of their sight.

[10]And while they looked stedfastly toward heaven as he went up, behold, two men stood by them in white apparel; [11]which also said, "Ye men of Galilee, why stand ye gazing up into heaven? This same Jesus, which is taken up from you into heaven, shall so come in like manner as ye have seen him go into heaven."

[12]Then returned they unto Jerusalem from the mount called Olivet, which is from Jerusalem a sabbath day's journey. [13]And when they were come in, they went up into an upper room, where abode both Peter, and James, and John, and Andrew, Philip, and Thomas, Bartholomew, and Matthew, James the son of Alphaeus, and Simon

THE ASCENSION *by Ambrogio Bondone Giotto*

Zelotes, and Judas the brother of James. [14]These all continued with one accord in prayer and supplication, with the women, and Mary the mother of Jesus, and with his brethren.

THE DAY OF PENTECOST

AND WHEN THE DAY OF PENTECOST WAS FULLY come, they were all with one accord in one place. [2]And suddenly there came a sound from heaven as of a rushing mighty wind, and it filled all the house where they were sitting. [3]And there appeared unto them cloven tongues like as of fire, and it sat upon each of them. [4]And they were all filled with the Holy Ghost, and began to speak with other tongues, as the Spirit gave them utterance.

[5]And there were dwelling at Jerusalem Jews, devout men, out of every nation under heaven. [6]Now when this was noised abroad, the multitude came together, and were confounded, because that every man heard them speak in his own language. [7]And they were all amazed and marvelled, saying one to another, "Behold, are not all these which speak Galilaeans? [8]And how hear we every man in our own tongue, wherein we were born? [9]Parthians, and Medes, and Elamites, and the dwellers in Mesopotamia, and in Judaea, and Cappadocia, in Pontus, and Asia, [10]Phrygia, and Pamphylia, in Egypt, and in the parts of Libya about Cyrene, and strangers of Rome, Jews and proselytes, [11]Cretes and Arabians, we do hear them speak in our tongues the wonderful works of God." [12]And they were all amazed, and were in doubt, saying one to another, "What meaneth this?"

[13]Others mocking said, "These men are full of new wine."

[14]But Peter, standing up with the eleven, lifted up his voice, and said unto them, "Ye men of Judaea, and all ye that dwell at Jerusalem, be this known unto you, and hearken to my words: [15]for these are not drunken, as ye suppose, seeing it is but the third hour of the day. [16]But this is that which was spoken by the prophet Joel:

[17]" 'And it shall come to pass in the last days, saith God,
I will pour out of my Spirit upon all flesh:
And your sons and your daughters shall prophesy,
And your young men shall see visions,
And your old men shall dream dreams:
[18]And on my servants and on my handmaidens
I will pour out in those days of my Spirit;
And they shall prophesy:
[19]And I will shew wonders in heaven above,
And signs in the earth beneath;
Blood, and fire, and vapour of smoke:
[20]The sun shall be turned into darkness,
And the moon into blood,
Before that great and notable day of the Lord come:

THE PENTECOST *by Louis Galloche*

[21]And it shall come to pass,
That whosoever shall call on the name of the Lord shall be saved."

[22]"Ye men of Israel, hear these words; Jesus of Nazareth, a man approved of God among you by miracles and wonders and signs, which God did by him in the midst of you, as ye

yourselves also know: [23]him, being delivered by the determinate counsel and foreknowledge of God, ye have taken, and by wicked hands have crucified and slain; [24]whom God hath raised up, having loosed the pains of death: because it was not possible that he should be holden of it. [25]For David speaketh concerning him,

"'I foresaw the Lord always before my face,
For he is on my right hand,
That I should not be moved:
[26]Therefore did my heart rejoice, and my tongue was glad;
Moreover also my flesh shall rest in hope:
[27]Because thou wilt not leave my soul in hell,
Neither wilt thou suffer thine Holy One to see corruption.
[28]Thou hast made known to me the ways of life;
Thou shalt make me full of joy with thy countenance.'

[29]"Men and brethren, let me freely speak unto you of the patriarch David, that he is both dead and buried, and his sepulchre is with us unto this day. [30]Therefore being a prophet, and knowing that God had sworn with an oath to him, that of the fruit of his loins, according to the flesh, he would raise up Christ to sit on his throne; [31]he seeing this before spake of the resurrection of Christ, that his soul was not left in hell, neither his flesh did see corruption. [32]This Jesus hath God raised up, whereof we all are witnesses. [33]Therefore being by the right hand of God exalted, and having received of the Father the promise of the Holy Ghost, he hath shed forth this, which ye now see and hear. [34]For David is not ascended into the heavens: but he saith himself,

"'The LORD said unto my Lord,
"Sit thou on my right hand,
[35]Until I make thy foes thy footstool."'

[36]"Therefore let all the house of Israel know assuredly, that God hath made that same Jesus, whom ye have crucified, both Lord and Christ."

[37]Now when they heard this, they were pricked in their heart, and said unto Peter and to the rest of the apostles, "Men and brethren, what shall we do?"

Chapter 2

[38]Then Peter said unto them, "Repent, and be baptized every one of you in the name of Jesus Christ for the remission of sins, and ye shall receive the gift of the Holy Ghost. [39]For the promise is unto you, and to your children, and to all that are afar off, even as many as the Lord our God shall call."

[40]And with many other words did he testify and exhort, saying, "Save yourselves from this untoward generation." [41]Then they that gladly received his word were baptized: and the same day there were added unto them about three thousand souls.

[42]And they continued stedfastly in the apostles' doctrine and fellowship, and in breaking of bread, and in prayers. [43]And fear came upon every soul: and many wonders and signs were done by the apostles. [44]And all that believed were together, and had all things common; [45]and sold their possessions and goods, and parted them to all men, as every man had need. [46]And they, continuing daily with one accord in the temple, and breaking bread from house to house, did eat their meat with gladness and singleness of heart, [47]praising God, and having favour with all the people. And the Lord added to the church daily such as should be saved.

The Healing at the Beautiful Gate

Chapter 3

Now Peter and John went up together into the temple at the hour of prayer, being the ninth hour. [2]And a certain man lame from his mother's womb was carried, whom they laid daily at the gate of the temple which is called Beautiful, to ask alms of them that entered into the temple; [3]who seeing Peter and John about to go into the temple asked an alms. [4]And Peter, fastening his eyes upon him with John, said, "Look on us." [5]And he gave heed unto them, expecting to receive something of them.

[6]Then Peter said, "Silver and gold have I none; but such as I have give I thee: in the name of Jesus Christ of Nazareth rise up and walk." [7]And he took him by the right

Chapter 3

hand, and lifted him up: and immediately his feet and ankle bones received strength. [8]And he leaping up stood, and walked, and entered with them into the temple, walking, and leaping, and praising God. [9]And all the people saw him walking and praising God: [10]and they all knew that it was he which sat for alms at the Beautiful gate of the temple: and they were filled with wonder and amazement at that which had happened unto him.

Ananias and Sapphira

Chapter 4

AND THE MULTITUDE OF THEM THAT BELIEVED were of one heart and of one soul: neither said any of them that aught of the things which he possessed was his own; but they had all things in common. [33]And with great power gave the apostles witness of the resurrection of the Lord Jesus: and great grace was upon them all. [34]Neither was there any among them that lacked: for as many as were possessors of lands or houses sold them, and brought the prices of the things that were sold, [35]and laid them down at the apostles'

THE DEATH OF ANANIAS *by Raphael*

Chapter 4

feet: and distribution was made unto every man according as he had need.

[36]And Joses, who by the apostles was surnamed Barnabas, (which is, being interpreted, The son of consolation,) a Levite, and of the country of Cyprus, [37]having land, sold it, and brought the money, and laid it at the apostles' feet.

Chapter 5

But a certain man named Ananias, with Sapphira his wife, sold a possession, [2]and kept back part of the price, his wife also being privy to it, and brought a certain part, and laid it at the apostles' feet.

[3]But Peter said, "Ananias, why hath Satan filled thine heart to lie to the Holy Ghost, and to keep back part of the price of the land? [4]Whiles it remained, was it not thine own? And after it was sold, was it not in thine own power? Why hast thou conceived this thing in thine heart? Thou hast not lied unto men, but unto God."

[5]And Ananias hearing these words fell down, and gave up the ghost: and great fear came on all them that heard these things. [6]And the young men arose, wound him up, and carried him out, and buried him.

[7]And it was about the space of three hours after, when his wife, not knowing what was done, came in. [8]And Peter answered unto her, "Tell me whether ye sold the land for so much?"

And she said, "Yea, for so much."

[9]Then Peter said unto her, "How is it that ye have agreed together to tempt the Spirit of the Lord? Behold, the feet of them which have buried thy husband are at the door, and shall carry thee out."

[10]Then fell she down straightway at his feet, and yielded up the ghost: and the young men came in, and found her dead, and, carrying her forth, buried her by her husband. [11]And great fear came upon all the church, and upon as many as heard these things.

The Choosing of the Seven

Chapter 6

AND IN THOSE DAYS, WHEN THE NUMBER OF THE disciples was multiplied, there arose a murmuring of the Grecians against the Hebrews, because their widows were neglected in the daily ministration. [2]Then the twelve called the multitude of the disciples unto them, and said, "It is not reason that we should leave the word of God, and serve tables. [3]Wherefore, brethren, look ye out among you seven men of honest report, full of the Holy Ghost and wisdom, whom we may appoint over this business. [4]But we will give ourselves continually to prayer, and to the ministry of the word."

[5]And the saying pleased the whole multitude: and they chose Stephen, a man full of faith and of the Holy Ghost, and Philip, and Prochorus, and Nicanor, and Timon, and Parmenas, and Nicolas a proselyte of Antioch: [6]whom they set before the apostles: and when they had prayed, they laid their hands on them.

St Stephen Preaching and St Stephen Addressing the Council *by Fra Angelico*

[7]And the word of God increased; and the number of the disciples multiplied in Jerusalem greatly; and a great company of the priests were obedient to the faith.

[8]And Stephen, full of faith and power, did great wonders and miracles among the people.

[9]Then there arose certain of the synagogue, which is called the synagogue of the Libertines, and Cyrenians, and Alexandrians, and of them of Cilicia and of Asia, disputing with Stephen.

[10]And they were not able to resist the wisdom and the spirit by which he spake.

[11]Then they suborned men, which said, "We have heard him speak blasphemous words against Moses, and against God."

[12]And they stirred up the people, and the elders, and the scribes, and came upon him, and caught him, and brought him to the council, [13]and set up false witnesses, which said, "This man ceaseth not to speak blasphemous words against this holy place, and the law: [14]for we have heard him say, that this Jesus of Nazareth shall destroy this place, and shall change the customs which Moses delivered us."

The Martyrdom of Stephen

Chapter 7

When they heard these things, they were cut to the heart, and they gnashed on him with their teeth. [55]But he, being full of the Holy Ghost, looked up stedfastly into heaven, and saw the glory of God, and Jesus standing on the right hand of God, [56]and said, "Behold, I see the heavens opened, and the Son of man standing on the right hand of God."

[57]Then they cried out with a loud voice, and stopped their ears, and ran upon him with one accord, [58]and cast him out of the city, and stoned him: and the witnesses laid down their clothes at a young man's feet, whose name was Saul.

Chapter 7

[59]And they stoned Stephen, calling upon God, and saying, "Lord Jesus, receive my spirit." [60]And he kneeled down, and cried with a loud voice, "Lord, lay not this sin to their charge." And when he had said this, he fell asleep.

Chapter 8

AND SAUL WAS CONSENTING UNTO HIS DEATH.

And at that time there was a great persecution against the church which was at Jerusalem; and they were all scattered abroad throughout the regions of Judaea and Samaria, except the apostles. [2]And devout men carried Stephen to his burial, and made great lamentation over him. [3]As for Saul, he made havoc of the church, entering into every house, and haling men and women committed them to prison.

[4]Therefore they that were scattered abroad went every where preaching the word.

PHILIP AND THE ETHIOPIAN EUNUCH

Chapter 8

AND THE ANGEL OF THE LORD SPAKE UNTO PHILIP, saying, "Arise, and go toward the south unto the way that goeth down from Jerusalem unto Gaza, which is desert." [27]And he arose and went: and, behold, a man of Ethiopia, an eunuch of great authority under Candace queen of the Ethiopians, who had the charge of all her treasure, and had come to Jerusalem for to worship, [28]was returning, and sitting in his chariot read Esaias the prophet. [29]Then the Spirit said unto Philip, "Go near, and join thyself to this chariot."

ST STEPHEN THE MARTYR *by Domenico Ghirlandaio*

[30]And Philip ran thither to him, and heard him read the prophet Esaias, and said, "Understandest thou what thou readest?"

[31]And he said, "How can I, except some man should guide me?" And he desired Philip that he would come up and sit with him.

[32]The place of the scripture which he read was this,

He was led as a sheep to the slaughter;
And like a lamb dumb before his shearer,
So opened he not his mouth:
[33]In his humiliation his judgment was taken away:
And who shall declare his generation?
For his life is taken from the earth.

[34]And the eunuch answered Philip, and said, "I pray thee, of whom speaketh the prophet this? Of himself, or of some other man?" [35]Then Philip opened his mouth, and began at the same scripture, and preached unto him Jesus.

[36]And as they went on their way, they came unto a certain water: and the eunuch said, "See, here is water; what doth hinder me to be baptized?"

St Philip Baptizing the Eunuch *by Jan Both*

Chapter 8

[37]And Philip said, "If thou believest with all thine heart, thou mayest."

And he answered and said, "I believe that Jesus Christ is the Son of God."

[38]And he commanded the chariot to stand still: and they went down both into the water, both Philip and the eunuch; and he baptized him. [39]And when they were come up out of the water, the Spirit of the Lord caught away Philip, that the eunuch saw him no more: and he went on his way rejoicing. [40]But Philip was found at Azotus: and passing through he preached in all the cities, till he came to Caesarea.

The Conversion of Saul

Chapter 9

AND SAUL, YET BREATHING OUT THREATENINGS and slaughter against the disciples of the Lord, went unto the high priest, [2]and desired of him letters to Damascus to the synagogues, that if he found any of this way, whether they were men or women, he might bring them bound unto Jerusalem. [3]And as he journeyed, he came near Damascus: and suddenly there shined round about him a light from heaven: [4]and he fell to the earth, and heard a voice saying unto him, "Saul, Saul, why persecutest thou me?"

[5]And he said, "Who art thou, Lord?"

And the Lord said, "I am Jesus whom thou persecutest; it is hard for thee to kick against the pricks."

[6]And he trembling and astonished said, "Lord, what wilt thou have me to do?"

And the Lord said unto him, "Arise, and go into the city, and it shall be told thee what thou must do."

[7]And the men which journeyed with him stood speechless, hearing a voice, but seeing no man. [8]And Saul arose from the earth; and when his eyes were opened, he saw no man: but they led him by the hand, and brought him into Damascus. [9]And he was three days without sight, and neither did eat nor drink.

[10]And there was a certain disciple at Damascus, named Ananias; and to him said the Lord in a vision, "Ananias."

And he said, "Behold, I am here, Lord."

[11]And the Lord said unto him, "Arise, and go into the street which is called Straight, and inquire in the house of Judas for one called Saul, of Tarsus; for, behold, he prayeth, [12]and hath seen in a vision a man named Ananias coming in, and putting his hand on him, that he might receive his sight."

[13]Then Ananias answered, "Lord, I have heard by many of this man, how much evil he hath done to thy saints at Jerusalem: [14]and here he hath authority from the chief priests to bind all that call on thy name."

[15]But the Lord said unto him, "Go thy way: for he is a chosen vessel unto me, to bear my name before the Gentiles, and kings, and the children of Israel: [16]for I will shew him how great things he must suffer for my name's sake."

[17]And Ananias went his way, and entered into the house; and putting his hands on him said, "Brother Saul, the Lord, even Jesus, that appeared unto thee in the way as thou camest, hath sent me, that thou mightest receive thy sight, and be filled with the Holy Ghost." [18]And immediately there fell from his eyes as it had been scales: and he received sight forthwith, and arose, and was baptized. [19]And when he had received meat, he was strengthened.

Then was Saul certain days with the disciples which were at Damascus. [20]And straightway he preached Christ in the synagogues, that he is the Son of God. [21]But all that heard him were amazed, and said; "Is not this he that destroyed them which called on this name in Jerusalem, and came hither for that intent, that he might bring them bound unto the chief priests?" [22]But Saul increased the more in strength, and confounded the Jews which dwelt at Damascus, proving that this is very Christ.

[23]And after that many days were fulfilled, the Jews took counsel to kill him: [24]but their laying await was known of Saul. And they watched the gates day and night to kill him. [25]Then the disciples took him by night, and let him down by the wall in a basket.

[26]And when Saul was come to Jerusalem, he assayed to join himself to the disciples: but they were all afraid of him, and believed not that he was a disciple. [27]But Barnabas

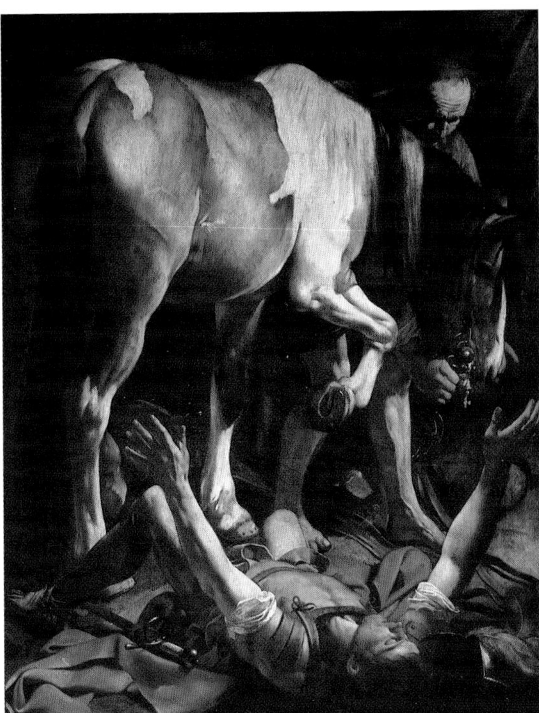

THE CONVERSION OF ST PAUL *by Caravaggio*

took him, and brought him to the apostles, and declared unto them how he had seen the Lord in the way, and that he had spoken to him, and how he had preached boldly at Damascus in the name of Jesus. [28]And he was with them coming in and going out at Jerusalem. [29]And he spake boldly in the name of the Lord Jesus, and disputed against the Grecians: but they went about to slay him. [30]Which when the brethren knew, they brought him down to Caesarea, and sent him forth to Tarsus.

Chapter 9

THE CONVERSION OF ST PAUL *by Jan Mostaert*

Chapter 9

[31]Then had the churches rest throughout all Judaea and Galilee and Samaria, and were edified; and walking in the fear of the Lord, and in the comfort of the Holy Ghost, were multiplied.

PETER AND CORNELIUS

Chapter 10

THERE WAS A CERTAIN MAN IN CAESAREA CALLED Cornelius, a centurion of the band called the Italian band, [2]a devout man, and one that feared God with all his house, which gave much alms to the people, and prayed to God alway. [3]He saw in a vision evidently about the ninth hour of the day an angel of God coming in to him, and saying unto him, "Cornelius."

[4]And when he looked on him, he was afraid, and said, "What is it, Lord?"

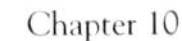

And he said unto him, "Thy prayers and thine alms are come up for a memorial before God. [5]And now send men to Joppa, and call for one Simon, whose surname is Peter: [6]he lodgeth with one Simon a tanner, whose house is by the sea side: he shall tell thee what thou oughtest to do."

[7]And when the angel which spake unto Cornelius was departed, he called two of his household servants, and a devout soldier of them that waited on him continually; [8]and when he had declared all these things unto them, he sent them to Joppa.

[9]On the morrow, as they went on their journey, and drew nigh unto the city, Peter went up upon the housetop to pray about the sixth hour: [10]and he became very hungry, and would have eaten: but while they made ready, he fell into a trance, [11]and saw heaven opened, and a certain vessel descending unto him, as it had been a great sheet knit at the four corners, and let down to the earth: [12]wherein were all manner of fourfooted beasts of the earth, and wild beasts, and creeping things, and fowls of the air. [13]And there came a voice to him, "Rise, Peter; kill, and eat."

[14]But Peter said, "Not so, Lord; for I have never eaten any thing that is common or unclean."

[15]And the voice spake unto him again the second time, "What God hath cleansed, that call not thou common."

[16]This was done thrice: and the vessel was received up again into heaven. [17]Now while Peter doubted in himself what this vision which he had seen should mean, behold, the men which were sent from Cornelius had made inquiry for Simon's house, and stood before the gate, [18]and called, and asked whether Simon, which was surnamed Peter, were lodged there.

[19]While Peter thought on the vision, the Spirit said unto him, "Behold, three men seek thee. [20]Arise therefore, and get thee down, and go with them, doubting nothing: for I have sent them."

[21]Then Peter went down to the men which were sent unto him from Cornelius; and said, "Behold, I am he whom ye seek: what is the cause wherefore ye are come?"

[22]And they said, Cornelius the centurion, a just man, and one that feareth God, and of good report among all the nation of the Jews, was warned from God by an holy angel

to send for thee to his house, and to hear words of thee." [23]Then called he them in, and lodged them.

And on the morrow Peter went away with them, and certain brethren from Joppa accompanied him. [24]And the morrow after they entered into Caesarea. And Cornelius waited for them, and had called together his kinsmen and near friends. [25]And as Peter was coming in, Cornelius met him, and fell down at his feet, and worshipped him. [26]But Peter took him up, saying, "Stand up; I myself also am a man."

[27]And as he talked with him, he went in, and found many that were come together. [28]And he said unto them, "Ye know how that it is an unlawful thing for a man that is a Jew to keep company, or come unto one of another nation; but God hath shewed me that I should not call any man common or unclean. [29]Therefore came I unto you without gainsaying, as soon as I was sent for: I ask therefore for what intent ye have sent for me?"

[30]And Cornelius said, "Four days ago I was fasting until this hour; and at the ninth hour I prayed in my house, and, behold, a man stood before me in bright clothing, [31]and said, Cornelius, thy prayer is heard, and thine alms are had in remembrance in the sight of God. [32]Send therefore to Joppa, and call hither Simon, whose surname is Peter; he is lodged in the house of one Simon a tanner by the sea side: who, when he cometh, shall speak unto thee.' [33]Immediately therefore I sent to thee; and thou hast well done that thou art come. Now therefore are we all here present before God, to hear all things that are commanded thee of God."

[34]Then Peter opened his mouth, and said, "Of a truth I perceive that God is no respecter of persons: [35]but in every nation he that feareth him, and worketh righteousness, is accepted with him. [36]The word which God sent unto the children of Israel, preaching peace by Jesus Christ: (he is Lord of all:) [37]that word, I say, ye know, which was published throughout all Judaea, and began from Galilee, after the baptism which John preached; [38]how God anointed Jesus of Nazareth with the Holy Ghost and with power: who went about doing good, and healing all that were oppressed of the devil; for God was with him.

Chapter 10

[39]"And we are witnesses of all things which he did both in the land of the Jews, and in Jerusalem; whom they slew and hanged on a tree: [40]him God raised up the third day, and shewed him openly; [41]not to all the people, but unto witnesses chosen before of God, even to us, who did eat and drink with him after he rose from the dead. [42]And he commanded us to preach unto the people, and to testify that it is he which was ordained of God to be the Judge of quick and dead. [43]To him give all the prophets witness, that through his name whosoever believeth in him shall receive remission of sins."

[44]While Peter yet spake these words, the Holy Ghost fell on all them which heard the word. [45]And they of the circumcision which believed were astonished, as many as came with Peter, because that on the Gentiles also was poured out the gift of the Holy Ghost. [46]For they heard them speak with tongues, and magnify God.

Then answered Peter, [47]"Can any man forbid water, that these should not be baptized, which have received the Holy Ghost as well as we?" [48]And he commanded them to be baptized in the name of the Lord. Then prayed they him to tarry certain days.

The Church in Antioch

Chapter 11

Now they which were scattered abroad upon the persecution that arose about Stephen travelled as far as Phenice, and Cyprus, and Antioch, preaching the word to none but unto the Jews only. [20]And some of them were men of Cyprus and Cyrene, which, when they were come to Antioch, spake unto the Grecians, preaching the Lord Jesus. [21]And the hand of the Lord was with them: and a great number believed, and turned unto the Lord.

[22]Then tidings of these things came unto the ears of the church which was in Jerusalem: and they sent forth Barnabas, that he should go as far as Antioch. [23]Who,

Chapter 11

when he came, and had seen the grace of God, was glad, and exhorted them all, that with purpose of heart they would cleave unto the Lord. [24]For he was a good man, and full of the Holy Ghost and of faith: and much people was added unto the Lord.

[25]Then departed Barnabas to Tarsus, for to seek Saul: [26]and when he had found him, he brought him unto Antioch. And it came to pass, that a whole year they assembled themselves with the church, and taught much people. And the disciples were called Christians first in Antioch.

Peter Delivered by an Angel

Chapter 12

Now about that time Herod the king stretched forth his hands to vex certain of the church. [2]And he killed James the brother of John with the sword. [3]And because he saw it pleased the Jews, he proceeded further to take Peter also. (Then were the days of unleavened bread.) [4]And when he had apprehended him, he put him in prison, and delivered him to four quaternions of soldiers to keep him; intending after Easter to bring him forth to the people.

[5]Peter therefore was kept in prison: but prayer was made without ceasing of the church unto God for him.

[6]And when Herod would have brought him forth, the same night Peter was sleeping between two soldiers, bound with two chains: and the keepers before the door kept the prison. [7]And, behold, the angel of the Lord came upon him, and a light shined in the prison: and he smote Peter on the side, and raised him up, saying, "Arise up quickly." And his chains fell off from his hands.

[8]And the angel said unto him, "Gird thyself, and bind on thy sandals." And so he did. And he saith unto him, "Cast thy garment about thee, and follow me." [9]And he went out, and followed him; and wist not that it was true which was done by the angel; but thought he saw a vision. [10]When they were past the first and the second ward, they

St Peter Released from Prison *by Filippo Vitale*

came unto the iron gate that leadeth unto the city; which opened to them of his own accord: and they went out, and passed on through one street: and forthwith the angel departed from him.

[11]And when Peter was come to himself, he said, "Now I know of a surety, that the Lord hath sent his angel, and hath delivered me out of the hand of Herod, and from all the expectation of the people of the Jews."

[12]And when he had considered the thing, he came to the house of Mary the mother of John, whose surname was Mark; where many were gathered together praying. [13]And as Peter knocked at the door of the gate, a damsel came to hearken, named Rhoda. [14]And when she knew Peter's voice, she opened not the gate for gladness, but ran in, and told how Peter stood before the gate.

[15]And they said unto her, "Thou art mad." But she constantly affirmed that it was even so. Then said they, "It is his angel."

[16]But Peter continued knocking: and when they had opened the door, and saw him, they were astonished. [17]But

Chapter 12

he, beckoning unto them with the hand to hold their peace, declared unto them how the Lord had brought him out of the prison. And he said, "Go shew these things unto James, and to the brethren." And he departed, and went into another place.

The Death of Herod

Chapter 12

NOW AS SOON AS IT WAS DAY, THERE WAS NO small stir among the soldiers, what was become of Peter. [19]And when Herod had sought for him, and found him not, he examined the keepers, and commanded that they should be put to death.

And he went down from Judaea to Caesarea, and there abode. [20]And Herod was highly displeased with them of Tyre and Sidon: but they came with one accord to him, and, having made Blastus the king's chamberlain their friend, desired peace; because their country was nourished by the king's country.

[21]And upon a set day Herod, arrayed in royal apparel, sat upon his throne, and made an oration unto them. [22]And the people gave a shout, saying, "It is the voice of a god, and not of a man." [23]And immediately the angel of the Lord smote him, because he gave not God the glory: and he was eaten of worms, and gave up the ghost.

[24]But the word of God grew and multiplied.

[25]And Barnabas and Saul returned from Jerusalem, when they had fulfilled their ministry, and took with them John, whose surname was Mark.

Chapter 13

NOW THERE WERE IN THE CHURCH THAT WAS AT ANTIOCH certain prophets and teachers; as Barnabas, and Simeon that was called Niger, and Lucius of Cyrene, and Manaen, which had been brought up with Herod the tetrarch, and

Chapter 13

Saul. [2]As they ministered to the Lord, and fasted, the Holy Ghost said, "Separate me Barnabas and Saul for the work whereunto I have called them." [3]And when they had fasted and prayed, and laid their hands on them, they sent them away.

Paul and Barnabas at Lystra

Chapter 14

AND THERE SAT A CERTAIN MAN AT LYSTRA, impotent in his feet, being a cripple from his mother's womb, who never had walked: [9]the same heard Paul speak: who stedfastly beholding him, and perceiving that he had faith to be healed, [10]said with a loud voice, "Stand upright on thy feet." And he leaped and walked.

[11]And when the people saw what Paul had done, they lifted up their voices, saying in the speech of Lycaonia, "The gods are come down to us in the likeness of men." [12]And they called Barnabas, Jupiter; and Paul, Mercurius, because he was the chief speaker. [13]Then the priest of Jupiter, which was before their city, brought oxen and

The Apostles, St Paul and St Barnabas at Lystra *by Jacob Jordaens*

Chapter 14

lands unto the gates, and would have done sacrifice with the people.

[14]Which when the apostles, Barnabas and Paul, heard of, they rent their clothes, and ran in among the people, crying out, [15]and saying, "Sirs, why do ye these things? We also are men of like passions with you, and preach unto you that ye should turn from these vanities unto the living God, which made heaven, and earth, and the sea, and all things that are therein: [16]who in times past suffered all nations to walk in their own ways. [17]Nevertheless he left not himself without witness, in that he did good, and gave us rain from heaven, and fruitful seasons, filling our hearts with food and gladness." [18]And with these sayings scarce restrained they the people, that they had not done sacrifice unto them.

[19]And there came thither certain Jews from Antioch and Iconium, who persuaded the people, and, having stoned Paul, drew him out of the city, supposing he had been dead. [20]Howbeit, as the disciples stood round about him, he rose up, and came into the city: and the next day he departed with Barnabas to Derbe.

[21]And when they had preached the gospel to that city, and had taught many, they returned again to Lystra, and to Iconium, and Antioch, [22]confirming the souls of the disciples, and exhorting them to continue in the faith, and that we must through much tribulation enter into the kingdom of God. [23]And when they had ordained them elders in every church, and had prayed with fasting, they commended them to the Lord, on whom they believed.

Paul's Vision of the Man of Macedonia

Chapter 15

AND SOME DAYS AFTER PAUL SAID UNTO BARNABAS, "Let us go again and visit our brethren in every city where we have preached the word of the Lord, and see how they do." [37]And Barnabas determined to take with them John, whose surname was Mark. [38]But Paul thought not

THE VISION OF ST PAUL, *Italian School*

Chapter 15 good to take him with them, who departed from them from Pamphylia, and went not with them to the work. [39]And the contention was so sharp between them, that they departed asunder one from the other: and so Barnabas took Mark, and sailed unto Cyprus; [40]and Paul chose Silas, and departed, being recommended by the brethren unto the grace of God. [41]And he went through Syria and Cilicia, confirming the churches.

Chapter 16 THEN CAME HE TO DERBE AND LYSTRA: AND, BEHOLD, A certain disciple was there, named Timotheus, the son of a certain woman, which was a Jewess, and believed; but his father was a Greek: [2]which was well reported of by the brethren that were at Lystra and Iconium. [3]Him would Paul have to go forth with him; and took and circumcised him because of the Jews which were in those quarters: for they knew all that his father was a Greek. [4]And as they went through the cities, they delivered them the decrees for to keep, that were ordained of the apostles and elders which were at Jerusalem. [5]And so were the churches established in the faith, and increased in number daily.

[6]Now when they had gone throughout Phrygia and the region of Galatia, and were forbidden of the Holy Ghost to preach the word in Asia, [7]after they were come to Mysia, they assayed to go into Bithynia: but the Spirit suffered them not. [8]And they passing by Mysia came down to Troas. [9]And a vision appeared to Paul in the night; there stood a man of Macedonia, and prayed him, saying, "Come over into Macedonia, and help us." [10]And after he had seen the vision, immediately we endeavoured to go into Macedonia, assuredly gathering that the Lord had called us for to preach the gospel unto them.

[11]Therefore loosing from Troas, we came with a straight course to Samothracia, and the next day to Neapolis; [12]and from thence to Philippi, which is the chief city of that part of Macedonia, and a colony: and we were in that city abiding certain days.

[13]And on the sabbath we went out of the city by a river side, where prayer was wont to be made; and we sat down, and spake unto the women which resorted thither. [14]And a

Chapter 16

certain woman named Lydia, a seller of purple, of the city of Thyatira, which worshipped God, heard us: whose heart the Lord opened, that she attended unto the things which were spoken of Paul. [15]And when she was baptized, and her household, she besought us, saying, "If ye have judged me to be faithful to the Lord, come into my house, and abide there." And she constrained us.

Paul Arrested

Chapter 19

AFTER THESE THINGS WERE ENDED, PAUL PURposed in the spirit, when he had passed through Macedonia and Achaia, to go to Jerusalem, saying, "After I have been there, I must also see Rome." . . .

Chapter 21

AND WHEN WE WERE COME TO JERUSALEM, THE BRETHREN received us gladly. [18]And the day following Paul went in with us unto James; and all the elders were present. [19]And when he had saluted them, he declared particularly what things God had wrought among the Gentiles by his ministry.

[20]And when they heard it, they glorified the Lord, and said unto him, "Thou seest, brother, how many thousands of Jews there are which believe; and they are all zealous of the law: [21]and they are informed of thee, that thou teachest all the Jews which are among the Gentiles to forsake Moses, saying that they ought not to circumcise their children, neither to walk after the customs. [22]What is it therefore? The multitude must needs come together: for they will hear that thou art come. [23]Do therefore this that we say to thee: We have four men which have a vow on them; [24]them take, and purify thyself with them, and be at charges with them, that they may shave their heads: and all may know that those things, whereof they were informed concerning thee, are nothing; but that thou thyself also

walkest orderly, and keepest the law. [25]As touching the Gentiles which believe, we have written and concluded that they observe no such thing, save only that they keep themselves from things offered to idols, and from blood, and from strangled, and from fornication."

[26]Then Paul took the men, and the next day purifying himself with them entered into the temple, to signify the accomplishment of the days of purification, until that an offering should be offered for every one of them.

[27]And when the seven days were almost ended, the Jews which were of Asia, when they saw him in the temple, stirred up all the people, and laid hands on him, [28]crying out, "Men of Israel, help: this is the man that teacheth all men every where against the people, and the law, and this place: and further brought Greeks also into the temple, and hath polluted this holy place." [29](For they had seen before with him in the city Trophimus an Ephesian, whom they supposed that Paul had brought into the temple.)

[30]And all the city was moved, and the people ran together: and they took Paul, and drew him out of the temple: and forthwith the doors were shut. [31]And as they went about to kill him, tidings came unto the chief captain of the band, that all Jerusalem was in an uproar. [32]Who immediately took soldiers and centurions, and ran down unto them: and when they saw the chief captain and the soldiers, they left beating of Paul.

[33]Then the chief captain came near, and took him, and commanded him to be bound with two chains; and demanded who he was, and what he had done. [34]And some cried one thing, some another, among the multitude: and when he could not know the certainty for the tumult, he commanded him to be carried into the castle.

Before the Sanhedrin

Chapter 22

On the morrow, because he would have known the certainty wherefore he was accused of the Jews, he loosed him from his bands, and commanded the chief priests and all their council to appear, and brought Paul down, and set him before them.

Chapter 23

And Paul, earnestly beholding the council, said, "Men and brethren, I have lived in all good conscience before God until this day." [2]And the high priest Ananias commanded them that stood by him to smite him on the mouth. [3]Then said Paul unto him, "God shall smite thee, thou whited wall: for sittest thou to judge me after the law, and commandest me to be smitten contrary to the law?"

[4]And they that stood by said, "Revilest thou God's high priest?"

St Paul Being Taken to his Martyrdom *by Luca di Tomme'*

Chapter 23

[5]Then said Paul, "I wist not, brethren, that he was the high priest: for it is written, 'Thou shalt not speak evil of the ruler of thy people.'"

[6]But when Paul perceived that the one part were Sadducees, and the other Pharisees, he cried out in the council, "Men and brethren, I am a Pharisee, the son of a Pharisee: of the hope and resurrection of the dead I am called in question." [7]And when he had so said, there arose a dissension between the Pharisees and the Sadducees: and the multitude was divided. [8]For the Sadducees say that there is no resurrection, neither angel, nor spirit: but the Pharisees confess both.

[9]And there arose a great cry: and the scribes that were of the Pharisees' part arose, and strove, saying, "We find no evil in this man: but if a spirit or an angel hath spoken to him, let us not fight against God." [10]And when there arose a great dissension, the chief captain, fearing lest Paul should have been pulled in pieces of them, commanded the soldiers to go down, and to take him by force from among them, and to bring him into the castle.

[11]And the night following the Lord stood by him, and said, "Be of good cheer, Paul: for as thou hast testified of me in Jerusalem, so must thou bear witness also at Rome."

The Plot to Kill Paul

Chapter 23

AND WHEN IT WAS DAY, CERTAIN OF THE JEWS banded together, and bound themselves under a curse, saying that they would neither eat nor drink till they had killed Paul. [13]And they were more than forty which had made this conspiracy. [14]And they came to the chief priests and elders, and said, "We have bound ourselves under a great curse, that we will eat nothing until we have slain Paul. [15]Now therefore ye with the council signify to the chief captain that he bring him down unto you to morrow, as though ye would inquire something more perfectly concerning him: and we, or ever he come near, are ready to kill him."

Chapter 23

[16]And when Paul's sister's son heard of their lying in wait, he went and entered into the castle, and told Paul.

[17]Then Paul called one of the centurions unto him, and said, "Bring this young man unto the chief captain: for he hath a certain thing to tell him."

[18]So he took him, and brought him to the chief captain, and said, "Paul the prisoner called me unto him, and prayed me to bring this young man unto thee, who hath something to say unto thee."

[19]Then the chief captain took him by the hand, and went with him aside privately, and asked him, "What is that thou hast to tell me?"

[20]And he said, "The Jews have agreed to desire thee that thou wouldest bring down Paul to morrow into the council, as though they would inquire somewhat of him more perfectly. [21]But do not thou yield unto them: for there lie in wait for him of them more than forty men, which have bound themselves with an oath, that they will neither eat nor drink till they have killed him: and now are they ready, looking for a promise from thee."

[22]So the chief captain then let the young man depart, and charged him, "See thou tell no man that thou hast shewed these things to me."

[23]And he called unto him two centurions, saying, "Make ready two hundred soldiers to go to Caesarea, and horsemen three score and ten, and spearmen two hundred, at the third hour of the night; [24]and provide them beasts, that they may set Paul on, and bring him safe unto Felix the governor."

BEFORE FELIX AND FESTUS

Chapter 24

AND AFTER CERTAIN DAYS, WHEN FELIX CAME with his wife Drusilla, which was a Jewess, he sent for Paul, and heard him concerning the faith in Christ. [25]And as he reasoned of righteousness, temperance, and judgment to come, Felix trembled, and answered, "Go thy way for

Chapter 24

this time: when I have a convenient season, I will call for thee." [26]He hoped also that money should have been given him of Paul, that he might loose him: wherefore he sent for him the oftener, and communed with him.

[27]But after two years Porcius Festus came into Felix' room: and Felix, willing to shew the Jews a pleasure, left Paul bound.

Chapter 25

NOW WHEN FESTUS WAS COME INTO THE PROVINCE, AFTER three days he ascended from Caesarea to Jerusalem. [2]Then the high priest and the chief of the Jews informed him against Paul, and besought him, [3]and desired favour against him, that he would send for him to Jerusalem, laying wait in the way to kill him. [4]But Festus answered, that Paul should be kept at Caesarea, and that he himself would depart shortly thither. [5]"Let them therefore," said he, "which among you are able, go down with me, and accuse this man, if there be any wickedness in him."

[6]And when he had tarried among them more than ten days, he went down unto Caesarea; and the next day sitting on the judgment seat commanded Paul to be brought. [7]And when he was come, the Jews which came down from Jerusalem stood round about, and laid many and grievous complaints against Paul, which they could not prove. [8]While he answered for himself, "Neither against the law of the Jews, neither against the temple, nor yet against Caesar, have I offended any thing at all."

[9]But Festus, willing to do the Jews a pleasure, answered Paul, and said, "Wilt thou go up to Jerusalem, and there be judged of these things before me?"

[10]Then said Paul, "I stand at Caesar's judgment seat, where I ought to be judged: to the Jews have I done no wrong, as thou very well knowest. [11]For if I be an offender, or have committed any thing worthy of death, I refuse not to die: but if there be none of these things whereof these accuse me, no man may deliver me unto them. I appeal unto Caesar."

[12]Then Festus, when he had conferred with the council, answered, "Hast thou appealed unto Caesar? Unto Caesar shalt thou go."

Paul's Voyage and Shipwreck

Chapter 27

AND WHEN IT WAS DETERMINED THAT WE SHOULD sail into Italy, they delivered Paul and certain other prisoners unto one named Julius, a centurion of Augustus' band. [2]And entering into a ship of Adramyttium, we launched, meaning to sail by the coasts of Asia; one Aristarchus, a Macedonian of Thessalonica, being with us.

[3]And the next day we touched at Sidon. And Julius courteously entreated Paul, and gave him liberty to go unto his friends to refresh himself. [4]And when we had launched from thence, we sailed under Cyprus, because the winds were contrary. [5]And when we had sailed over the sea of Cilicia and Pamphylia, we came to Myra, a city of Lycia. [6]And there the centurion found a ship of Alexandria sailing into Italy; and he put us therein. [7]And when we had sailed slowly many days, and scarce were come over against Cnidus, the wind not suffering us, we sailed under Crete, over against Salmone; [8]and, hardly passing it, came unto a place which is called The fair havens; nigh whereunto was the city of Lasea.

[9]Now when much time was spent, and when sailing was now dangerous, because the fast was now already past, Paul admonished them, [10]and said unto them, "Sirs, I perceive that this voyage will be with hurt and much damage, not only of the lading and ship, but also of our lives." [11]Nevertheless the centurion believed the master and the owner of the ship, more than those things which were spoken by Paul. [12]And because the haven was not commodious to winter in, the more part advised to depart thence also, if by any means they might attain to Phenice, and there to winter: which is an haven of Crete, and lieth toward the south west and north west.

[13]And when the south wind blew softly, supposing that they had obtained their purpose, loosing thence, they sailed close by Crete. [14]But not long after there arose against it a tempestuous wind, called Euroclydon. [15]And when the ship was caught, and could not bear up into the wind, we let her drive. [16]And running under a certain

EMBARKATION OF ST PAUL AT OSTIA *by Claude Lorrain*

island which is called Clauda, we had much work to come by the boat: [17]which when they had taken up, they used helps, undergirding the ship; and, fearing lest they should fall into the quicksands, strake sail, and so were driven. [18]And we being exceedingly tossed with a tempest, the next day they lightened the ship; [19]and the third day we cast out with our own hands the tackling of the ship. [20]And

when neither sun nor stars in many days appeared, and no small tempest lay on us, all hope that we should be saved was then taken away.

[21]But after long abstinence Paul stood forth in the midst of them, and said, "Sirs, ye should have hearkened unto me, and not have loosed from Crete, and to have gained this harm and loss. [22]And now I exhort you to be of good cheer: for there shall be no loss of any man's life among you, but of the ship. [23]For there stood by me this night the angel of God, whose I am, and whom I serve, [24]saying, 'Fear not, Paul; thou must be brought before Caesar: and, lo, God hath given thee all them that sail with thee.' [25]Wherefore, sirs, be of good cheer: for I believe God, that it shall be even as it was told me. [26]Howbeit we must be cast upon a certain island."

[27]But when the fourteenth night was come, as we were driven up and down in Adria, about midnight the shipmen deemed that they drew near to some country; [28]and sounded, and found it twenty fathoms: and when they had gone a little further, they sounded again, and found it fifteen fathoms. [29]Then fearing lest we should have fallen upon rocks, they cast four anchors out of the stern, and wished for the day. [30]And as the shipmen were about to flee out of the ship, when they had let down the boat into the sea, under colour as though they would have cast anchors out of the foreship, [31]Paul said to the centurion and to the soldiers, "Except these abide in the ship, ye cannot be saved." [32]Then the soldiers cut off the ropes of the boat, and let her fall off.

[33]And while the day was coming on, Paul besought them all to take meat, saying, "This day is the fourteenth day that ye have tarried and continued fasting, having taken nothing. [34]Wherefore I pray you to take some meat: for this is for your health: for there shall not an hair fall from the head of any of you." [35]And when he had thus spoken, he took bread, and gave thanks to God in presence of them all: and when he had broken it, he began to eat. [36]Then were they all of good cheer, and they also took some meat. [37]And we were all in the ship two hundred threescore and sixteen souls. [38]And when they had eaten enough, they lightened the ship, and cast out the wheat into the sea.

Chapter 27

[39]And when it was day, they knew not the land: but they discovered a certain creek with a shore, into the which they were minded, if it were possible, to thrust in the ship. [40]And when they had taken up the anchors, they committed themselves unto the sea, and loosed the rudder bands, and hoised up the mainsail to the wind, and made toward shore. [41]And falling into a place where two seas met, they ran the ship aground; and the forepart stuck fast, and remained unmoveable, but the hinder part was broken with the violence of the waves.

[42]And the soldiers' counsel was to kill the prisoners, lest any of them should swim out, and escape. [43]But the centurion, willing to save Paul, kept them from their purpose; and commanded that they which could swim should cast themselves first into the sea, and get to land: [44]and the rest, some on boards, and some on broken pieces of the ship. And so it came to pass, that they escaped all safe to land.

Chapter 28

AND WHEN THEY WERE ESCAPED, THEN THEY KNEW THAT the island was called Melita. [2]And the barbarous people shewed us no little kindness: for they kindled a fire, and received us every one, because of the present rain, and because of the cold. [3]And when Paul had gathered a bundle of sticks, and laid them on the fire, there came a viper out of the heat, and fastened on his hand. [4]And when the barbarians saw the venomous beast hang on his hand, they said among themselves, "No doubt this man is a murderer, whom, though he hath escaped the sea, yet vengeance suffered not to live." [5]And he shook off the beast into the fire, and felt no harm. [6]Howbeit they looked when he should have swollen, or fallen down dead suddenly: but after they had looked a great while, and saw no harm come to him, they changed their minds, and said that he was a god.

[7]In the same quarters were possessions of the chief man of the island, whose name was Publius; who received us, and lodged us three days courteously. [8]And it came to pass, that the father of Publius lay sick of a fever and of a bloody flux: to whom Paul entered in, and prayed, and laid his

Chapter 28

St Paul Arriving at Malta *by Pieter Mulier*

hands on him, and healed him. [9]So when this was done, others also, which had diseases in the island, came, and were healed: [10]who also honoured us with many honours; and when we departed, they laded us with such things as were necessary.

[11]And after three months we departed in a ship of Alexandria, which had wintered in the isle, whose sign was Castor and Pollux.

Chapter 28

Paul in Rome

And when we came to Rome, the centurion delivered the prisoners to the captain of the guard: but Paul was suffered to dwell by himself with a soldier that kept him.

[17]And it came to pass, that after three days Paul called the chief of the Jews together: and when

Chapter 28

they were come together, he said unto them, "Men and brethren, though I have committed nothing against the people, or customs of our fathers, yet was I delivered prisoner from Jerusalem into the hands of the Romans. [18]Who, when they had examined me, would have let me go, because there was no cause of death in me. [19]But when the Jews spake against it, I was constrained to appeal unto Caesar; not that I had aught to accuse my nation of. [20]For this cause therefore have I called for you, to see you, and to speak with you: because that for the hope of Israel I am bound with this chain."

[21]And they said unto him, "We neither received letters out of Judaea concerning thee, neither any of the brethren that came shewed or spake any harm of thee. [22]But we desire to hear of thee what thou thinkest: for as concerning this sect, we know that every where it is spoken against."

[23]And when they had appointed him a day, there came many to him into his lodging; to whom he expounded and testified the kingdom of God, persuading them concerning Jesus, both out of the law of Moses, and out of the prophets, from morning till evening. [24]And some believed the things which were spoken, and some believed not. [25]And when they agreed not among themselves, they departed, after that Paul had spoken one word, "Well spake the Holy Ghost by Esaias the prophet unto our fathers, [26]saying,

"'Go unto this people, and say,
'Hearing ye shall hear, and shall not understand;
And seeing ye shall see, and not perceive":
[27]For the heart of this people is waxed gross,
And their ears are dull of hearing,
And their eyes have they closed;
Lest they should see with their eyes,
And hear with their ears,
And understand with their heart,
And should be converted, and I should heal them.'

[28]"Be it known therefore unto you, that the salvation of God is sent unto the Gentiles, and that they will hear it." [29]And when he had said these words, the Jews departed, and had great reasoning among themselves.

THE PREDICTION OF ST. PAUL *by Luca di Tomme'*

[30]And Paul dwelt two whole years in his own hired house, and received all that came in unto him, [31]preaching the kingdom of God, and teaching those things which concern the Lord Jesus Christ, with all confidence, no man forbidding him.

Chapter & Verses
FROM

THE
EPISTLES OF
ST. PAUL

AND THE

GENERAL EPISTLES

LORD IN MAJESTY detail from Ghent Altarpiece *by Jan van Eyck*

The Epistle of Paul to the Romans

Paul's longing to visit Rome • peace and joy • the law of the spirit • more than conquerors • glory to god • a living sacrifice • love the fulfilling of the law

—— • ——

The First Epistle of Paul to The Corinthians

paul's plea for unity • paul's self-denial • warnings from israel's history • spiritual gifts • the excellence of charity • the truth of the resurrection • at the Last trump

—— • ——

The Second Epistle of Paul to The Corinthians

the ministry of reconciliation • generosity encouraged

—— • ——

The Epistle of Paul to The Galatians

justification by faith • law and faith • the fruits of the spirit

—— • ——

The Epistle of Paul to The Ephesians

the riches of christ's glory • paul's prayer for the ephesians • the armour of god

—— • ——

The Epistle of Paul to The Philippians

the example of christ • paul's loss for christ • "rejoice in the lord"

—— • ——

The Epistle of Paul to The Colossians

paul's prayer for the colossians • risen with christ

— • —

The First Epistle of Paul to The Thessalonians

THE COMING OF THE LORD • EXHORTATIONS TO HOLY LIVING

— • —

The First Epistle of Paul to Timothy

THE LORD'S MERCY TO PAUL • THE LOVE OF MONEY

—————— • ——————

The Second Epistle of Paul to Timothy

THE SOLDIER OF CHRIST • PAUL'S CHARGE TO TIMOTHY

—————— • ——————

The Epistle of Paul to The Hebrews

THE SON SUPERIOR TO ANGELS • JESUS GREATER THAN MOSES • JESUS THE GREAT HIGH PRIEST • EXAMPLES OF FAITH • THE EXAMPLE OF JESUS • THE HEAVENLY JERUSALEM • LOVE AND CONTENTMENT • A PRAYER FOR THE HEBREWS

—————— • ——————

The General Epistle of James

HEARING AND DOING • FAITH AND WORKS

—————— • ——————

The First Epistle General of Peter

A LIVELY HOPE • A CHOSEN PEOPLE • GOOD STEWARDSHIP

– • –

The Second Epistle General of Peter

PETER'S TESTIMONY • THE DAY OF THE LORD

—————— • ——————

The First Epistle General of John

GOD IS LIGHT • SONS OF GOD • GOD IS LOVE

—————— • ——————

The General Epistle of Jude

DOXOLOGY

THE EPISTLE OF PAUL THE APOSTLE TO

THE ROMANS

Paul's Longing to Visit Rome

Chapter 1

PAUL, A SERVANT OF JESUS CHRIST, CALLED TO BE an apostle, separated unto the gospel of God, [2](which he had promised afore by his prophets in the holy scriptures,) [3]concerning his Son Jesus Christ our Lord, which was made of the seed of David according to the flesh; [4]and declared to be the Son of God with power, according to the spirit of holiness, by the resurrection from the dead: [5]by whom we have received grace and apostleship, for obedience to the faith among all nations, for his name: [6]among whom are ye also the called of Jesus Christ:

[7]To all that be in Rome, beloved of God, called to be saints:

Grace to you and peace from God our Father, and the Lord Jesus Christ.

Chapter 1

[8]First, I thank my God through Jesus Christ for you all, that your faith is spoken of throughout the whole world. [9]For God is my witness, whom I serve with my spirit in the gospel of his Son, that without ceasing I make mention of you always in my prayers; [10]making request, if by any means now at length I might have a prosperous journey by the will of God to come unto you.

[11]For I long to see you, that I may impart unto you some spiritual gift, to the end ye may be established; [12]that is, that I may be comforted together with you by the mutual faith both of you and me. [13]Now I would not have you ignorant, brethren, that oftentimes I purposed to come unto you, (but was let hitherto,) that I might have some fruit among you also, even as among other Gentiles.

[14]I am debtor both to the Greeks and to the Barbarians; both to the wise, and to the unwise. [15]So, as much as in me is, I am ready to preach the gospel to you that are at Rome also.

[16]For I am not ashamed of the gospel of Christ: for it is the power of God unto salvation to every one that believeth; to the Jew first, and also to the Greek. [17]For therein is the righteousness of God revealed from faith to faith: as it is written, "The just shall live by faith."

Peace and Joy

Chapter 5

THEREFORE BEING JUSTIFIED BY FAITH, WE HAVE peace with God through our Lord Jesus Christ: [2]by whom also we have access by faith into this grace wherein we stand, and rejoice in hope of the glory of God. [3]And not only so, but we glory in tribulations also: knowing that tribulation worketh patience; [4]and patience, experience; and experience, hope: [5]and hope maketh not ashamed; because the love of God is shed abroad in our hearts by the Holy Ghost which is given unto us.

[6]For when we were yet without strength, in due time Christ died for the ungodly. [7]For scarcely for a righteous man will one die: yet peradventure for a good man some

Chapter 5

would even dare to die. [8]But God commendeth his love toward us, in that, while we were yet sinners, Christ died for us.

[9]Much more then, being now justified by his blood, we shall be saved from wrath through him. [10]For if we were enemies, we were reconciled to God by the death of his Son, much more, being reconciled, we shall be saved by his life. [11]And not only so, but we also joy in God through our Lord Jesus Christ, by whom we have now received the atonement.

The Law of the Spirit

Chapter 8

THERE IS THEREFORE NOW NO CONDEMNATION to them which are in Christ Jesus, who walk not after the flesh, but after the Spirit. [2]For the law of the Spirit of life in Christ Jesus hath made me free from the law of sin and death. [3]For what the law could not do, in that it was weak through the flesh, God sending his own son in the likeness of sinful flesh, and for sin, condemned sin in the flesh: [4]that the righteousness of the law might be fulfilled in us, who walk not after the flesh, but after the Spirit.

[5]For they that are after the flesh do mind the things of the flesh; but they that are after the Spirit the things of the Spirit. [6]For to be carnally minded is death; but to be spiritually minded is life and peace. [7]Because the carnal mind is enmity against God: for it is not subject to the law of God, neither indeed can be. [8]So then they that are in the flesh cannot please God.

[9]But ye are not in the flesh, but in the Spirit, if so be that the Spirit of God dwell in you. Now if any man have not the Spirit of Christ, he is none of his. [10]And if Christ be in you, the body is dead because of sin; but the Spirit is life because of righteousness. [11]But if the Spirit of him that raised up Jesus from the dead dwell in you, he that raised up Christ from the dead shall also quicken your mortal bodies by his Spirit that dwelleth in you.

THE BATTLE OF LOVE AND CHASTITY *by Pietro Perugino*

[12]Therefore, brethren, we are debtors, not to the flesh, to live after the flesh. [13]For if ye live after the flesh, ye shall die: but if ye through the Spirit do mortify the deeds of the body, ye shall live. [14]For as many as are led by the Spirit of God, they are the sons of God. [15]For ye have not received the spirit of bondage again to fear; but ye have received the Spirit of adoption, whereby we cry, "Abba, Father." [16]The Spirit itself beareth witness with our spirit, that we are the children of God: [17]and if children, then heirs; heirs of God, and joint-heirs with Christ; if so be that we suffer with him, that we may be also glorified together. [18]For I reckon that the sufferings of this present time are not worthy to be compared with the glory which shall be revealed in us.

More Than Conquerors

Chapter 8

WHAT SHALL WE THEN SAY TO THESE things? If God be for us, who can be against us? [32]He that spared not his own Son, but delivered him up for us all, how shall he not with him also freely give us all things? [33]Who shall lay any thing to the charge of God's elect? It is God that justifieth. [34]Who is he that condemneth? It is Christ that died, yea rather, that is risen again, who is even at the right hand of God, who also maketh intercession for us.

[35]Who shall separate us from the love of Christ? Shall tribulation, or distress, or persecution, or famine, or nakedness, or peril, or sword? [36]As it is written, "For thy sake we are killed all the day long; we are accounted as sheep for the slaughter." [37]Nay, in all these things we are more than conquerors through him that loved us. [38]For I am persuaded, that neither death, nor life, nor angels, nor principalities, nor powers, nor things present, nor things to come, [39]nor height, nor depth, nor any other creature, shall be able to separate us from the love of God, which is in Christ Jesus our Lord.

Glory to God

Chapter 11

O THE DEPTH OF THE RICHES BOTH OF THE wisdom and knowledge of God!
How unsearchable are his judgments,
And his ways past finding out!
[34]For who hath known the mind of the Lord?
Or who hath been his counsellor?
[35]Or who hath first given to him,
And it shall be recompensed unto him again?
[36]For of him, and through him, and to him, are all things:
To whom be glory for ever. Amen.

A Living Sacrifice

Chapter 12

I BESEECH YOU THEREFORE, BRETHREN, BY THE MERCIES of God, that ye present your bodies a living sacrifice, holy, acceptable unto God, which is your reasonable service. [2]And be not conformed to this world: but be ye transformed by the renewing of your mind, that ye may prove what is that good, and acceptable, and perfect, will of God.

[3]For I say, through the grace given unto me, to every man that is among you, not to think of himself more highly than he ought to think; but to think soberly, according as God hath dealt to every man the measure of faith. [4]For as we have many members in one body, and all members have not the same office: [5]so we, being many, are one body in Christ, and every one members one of another. [6]Having then gifts differing according to the grace that is given to us, whether prophecy, let us prophesy according to the proportion of faith; [7]or ministry, let us wait on our ministering: or he that teacheth, on teaching; [8]or he that exhorteth, on exhortation: he that giveth, let him do it with simplicity; he that ruleth, with diligence; he that sheweth mercy, with cheerfulness.

[9]Let love be without dissimulation. Abhor that which is evil; cleave to that which is good. [10]Be kindly affectioned one to another with brotherly love; in honour preferring one another; [11]not slothful in business; fervent in spirit; serving the Lord; [12]rejoicing in hope; patient in tribulation; continuing instant in prayer; [13]distributing to the necessity of saints; given to hospitality.

[14]Bless them which persecute you: bless, and curse not. [15]Rejoice with them that do rejoice, and weep with them that weep. [16]Be of the same mind one toward another. Mind not high things, but condescend to men of low estate. Be not wise in your own conceits.

[17]Recompense to no man evil for evil. Provide things honest in the sight of all men. [18]If it be possible, as much as lieth in you, live peaceably with all men. [19]Dearly beloved, avenge not yourselves, but rather give place unto wrath: for it is written, "Vengeance is mine; I will repay," saith the

Chapter 12

Lord. [20]Therefore "if thine enemy hunger, feed him; if he thirst, give him drink: for in so doing thou shalt heap coals of fire on his head." [21]Be not overcome of evil, but overcome evil with good.

Love the Fulfilling of the Law

Chapter 13

WE NO MAN ANY THING, BUT TO LOVE ONE another: for he that loveth another hath fulfilled the law. [9]For this, "Thou shalt not commit adultery", "Thou shalt not kill", "Thou shalt not steal", "Thou shalt not

Detail from The Ten Commandments *by Lucas Cranach*

covet"; and if there be any other commandment, it is briefly comprehended in this saying, namely, "Thou shalt love thy neighbour as thyself." [10]Love worketh no ill to his neighbour: therefore love is the fulfilling of the law.

[11]And that, knowing the time, that now it is high time to awake out of sleep: for now is our salvation nearer than when we believed.

[12]The night is far spent, the day is at hand: let us therefore cast off the works of darkness, and let us put on the armour of light.

[13]Let us walk honestly, as in the day; not in rioting and drunkenness, not in chambering and wantonness, not in strife and envying. [14]But put ye on the Lord Jesus Christ, and make not provision for the flesh, to fulfil the lusts thereof.

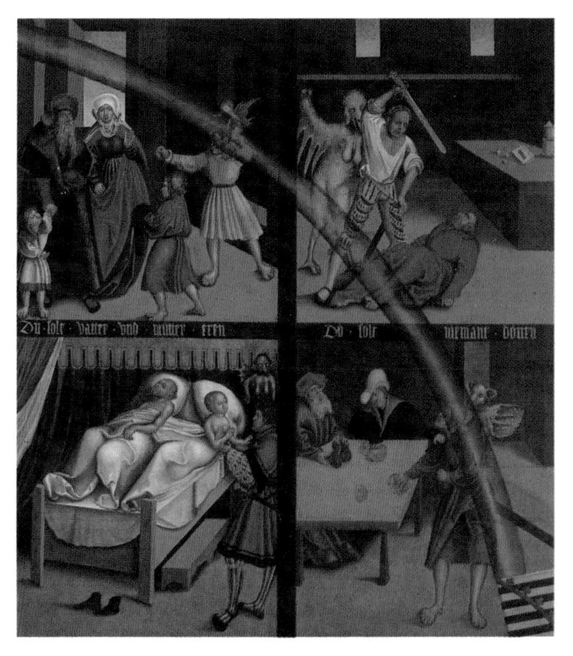

Detail from The Ten Commandments *by Lucas Cranach*

THE FIRST EPISTLE OF
PAUL THE APOSTLE TO

THE CORINTHIANS

Paul's Plea for Unity

Chapter 1

NOW I BESEECH YOU, BRETHREN, BY THE NAME of our Lord Jesus Christ, that ye all speak the same thing, and that there be no divisions among you; but that ye be perfectly joined together in the same mind and in the same judgment. 11For it hath been declared unto me of you, my brethren, by them which are of the house of Chloe, that there are contentions among you. 12Now this I say, that every one of you saith, "I am of Paul"; and "I of Apollos"; and "I of Cephas"; and "I of Christ."

13Is Christ divided? Was Paul crucified for you? Or were ye baptized in the name of Paul? 14I thank God that I baptized none of you, but Crispus and Gaius; 15lest any should say that I had baptized in mine own name. 16And I baptized also the household of Stephanas: besides, I know not whether I baptized any other. 17For Christ sent me not to baptize, but to preach the gospel: not with wisdom of words, lest the cross of Christ should be made of none effect.

Chapter 1

[18]For the preaching of the cross is to them that perish foolishness; but unto us which are saved it is the power of God. [19]For it is written, "I will destroy the wisdom of the wise, and will bring to nothing the understanding of the prudent." [20]Where is the wise? Where is the scribe? Where is the disputer of this world? Hath not God made foolish the wisdom of this world? [21]For after that in the wisdom of God the world by wisdom knew not God, it pleased God by the foolishness of preaching to save them that believe. [22]For the Jews require a sign, and the Greeks seek after wisdom; [23]but we preach Christ crucified, unto the Jews a stumblingblock, and unto the Greeks foolishness; [24]but unto them which are called, both Jews and Greeks, Christ the power of God, and the wisdom of God. [25]Because the foolishness of God is wiser than men; and the weakness of God is stronger than men.

Paul's Self-Denial

Chapter 9

DO YE NOT KNOW THAT THEY WHICH MINISTER about holy things live of the things of the temple? And they which wait at the altar are partakers with the altar? [14]Even so hath the Lord ordained that they which preach the gospel should live of the gospel.

[15]But I have used none of these things: neither have I written these things, that it should be so done unto me: for it were better for me to die, than that any man should make my glorying void. [16]For though I preach the gospel, I have nothing to glory of: for necessity is laid upon me; yea, woe is unto me, if I preach not the gospel! [17]For if I do this thing willingly, I have a reward: but if against my will, a dispensation of the gospel is committed unto me. [18]What is my reward then? Verily that, when I preach the gospel, I may make the gospel of Christ without charge, that I abuse not my power in the gospel.

[19]For though I be free from all men, yet have I made myself servant unto all, that I might gain the more. [20]And

Chapter 9

unto the Jews I became as a Jew, that I might gain the Jews; to them that are under the law, as under the law, that I might gain them that are under the law; [21]to them that are without law, as without law, (being not without law to God, but under the law to Christ,) that I might gain them that are without law. [22]To the weak became I as weak, that I might gain the weak: I am made all things to all men, that I might by all means save some. [23]And this I do for the gospel's sake, that I might be partaker thereof with you.

[24]Know ye not that they which run in a race run all, but one receiveth the prize? So run, that ye may obtain. [25]And every man that striveth for the mastery is temperate in all things. Now they do it to obtain a corruptible crown; but we an incorruptible. [26]I therefore so run, not as uncertainly; so fight I, not as one that beateth the air: [27]but I keep under my body, and bring it into subjection: lest that by any means, when I have preached to others, I myself should be a castaway.

Warnings From Israel's History

Chapter 10

MOREOVER, BRETHREN, I WOULD NOT THAT ye should be ignorant, how that all our fathers were under the cloud, and all passed through the sea; [2]and were all baptized unto Moses in the cloud and in the sea; [3]and did all eat the same spiritual meat; [4]and did all drink the same spiritual drink: for they drank of that spiritual Rock that followed them: and that Rock was Christ. [5]But with many of them God was not well pleased: for they were overthrown in the wilderness.

[6]Now these things were our examples, to the intent we should not lust after evil things, as they also lusted. [7]Neither be ye idolaters, as were some of them; as it is written, "The people sat down to eat and drink, and rose up to play." [8]Neither let us commit fornication, as some of them committed, and fell in one day three and twenty thousand. [9]Neither let us tempt Christ, as some of them also tempted,

MOSES STRIKING THE ROCK *by Jacopo Tintoretto*

Chapter 10

and were destroyed of serpents. [10]Neither murmur ye, as some of them also murmured, and were destroyed of the destroyer.

[11]Now all these things happened unto them for ensamples: and they are written for our admonition, upon whom the ends of the world are come. [12]Wherefore let him that thinketh he standeth take heed lest he fall. [13]There hath no temptation taken you but such as is common to man: but God is faithful, who will not suffer you to be tempted above that ye are able; but will with the temptation also make a way to escape, that ye may be able to bear it. [14]Wherefore, my dearly beloved, flee from idolatry. [15]I speak as to wise men; judge ye what I say. [16]The cup of blessing which we bless, is it not the communion of the blood of Christ? The bread which we break, is it not the communion of the body of Christ? [17]For we being many are one bread, and one body: for we are all partakers of that one bread.

Spiritual Gifts

Chapter 12

NOW CONCERNING SPIRITUAL GIFTS, BRETHren, I would not have you ignorant. [2]Ye know that ye were Gentiles, carried away unto these dumb idols, even as ye were led. [3]Wherefore I give you to understand, that no man speaking by the Spirit of God calleth Jesus accursed: and that no man can say that Jesus is the Lord, but by the Holy Ghost.

[4]Now there are diversities of gifts, but the same Spirit. [5]And there are differences of administrations, but the same Lord. [6]And there are diversities of operations, but it is the same God which worketh all in all.

[7]But the manifestation of the Spirit is given to every man to profit withal. [8]For to one is given by the Spirit the word of wisdom; to another the word of knowledge by the same Spirit; [9]to another faith by the same Spirit; to another the gifts of healing by the same Spirit; [10]to another the working of miracles; to another prophecy; to another discerning of spirits; to another divers kinds of tongues; to another the interpretation of tongues: [11]but all these worketh that one and the selfsame Spirit, dividing to every man severally as he will.

[12]For as the body is one, and hath many members, and all the members of that one body, being many, are as one body: so also is Christ. [13]For by one Spirit are we all baptized into one body, whether we be Jews or Gentiles, whether we be bond or free; and have been all made to drink into one Spirit. [14]For the body is not one member, but many. [15]If the foot shall say, "Because I am not the hand, I am not of the body"; is it therefore not of the body? [16]And if the ear shall say, "Because I am not the eye, I am not of the body"; is it therefore not of the body? [17]If the whole body were an eye, where were the hearing? If the whole were hearing, where were the smelling? [18]But now hath God set the members every one of them in the body, as it hath pleased him. [19]And if they were all one member, where were the body? [20]But now are they many members, yet but one body.

Chapter 12

[21]And the eye cannot say unto the hand, "I have no need of thee"; nor again the head to the feet, "I have no need of you." [22]Nay, much more those members of the body, which seem to be more feeble, are necessary: [23]and those members of the body, which we think to be less honourable, upon these we bestow more abundant honour; and our uncomely parts have more abundant comeliness. [24]For our comely parts have no need: but God hath tempered the body together, having given more abundant honour to that part which lacked: [25]that there should be no schism in the body; but that the members should have the same care one for another. [26]And whether one member suffer, all the members suffer with it; or one member be honoured, all the members rejoice with it.

[27]Now ye are the body of Christ, and members in particular. [28]And God hath set some in the church, first apostles, secondarily prophets, thirdly teachers, after that miracles, then gifts of healings, helps, governments, diversities of tongues. [29]Are all apostles? Are all prophets? Are all teachers? Are all workers of miracles? [30]Have all the gifts of healing? Do all speak with tongues? Do all interpret? [31]But covet earnestly the best gifts: and yet shew I unto you a more excellent way.

The Excellence of Charity

Chapter 13

THOUGH I SPEAK WITH THE TONGUES OF MEN and of angels, and have not charity, I am become as sounding brass, or a tinkling cymbal. [2]And though I have the gift of prophecy, and understand all mysteries, and all knowledge; and though I have all faith, so that I could remove mountains, and have not charity, I am nothing. [3]And though I bestow all my goods to feed the poor, and though I give my body to be burned, and have not charity, it profiteth me nothing.

[4]Charity suffereth long, and is kind; charity envieth not; charity vaunteth not itself, is not puffed up, [5]doth not

CHARITY DISPENSING ALMS *by Giovanni-Battista Tiepolo*

behave itself unseemly, seeketh not her own, is not easily provoked, thinketh no evil; [6]rejoiceth not in iniquity, but rejoiceth in the truth; [7]beareth all things, believeth all things, hopeth all things, endureth all things.

[8]Charity never faileth: but whether there be prophecies, they shall fail; whether there be tongues, they shall cease; whether there be knowledge, it shall vanish away. [9]For we know in part, and we prophesy in part. [10]But when that which is perfect is come, then that which is in part shall be done away. [11]When I was a child, I spake as a child, I

Chapter 13

understood as a child, I thought as a child: but when I became a man, I put away childish things. [12]For now we see through a glass, darkly; but then face to face: now I know in part; but then shall I know even as also I am known.

[13]And now abideth faith, hope, charity, these three; but the greatest of these is charity.

The Truth of the Resurrection

Chapter 15

MOREOVER, BRETHREN, I DECLARE UNTO YOU the gospel which I preached unto you, which also ye have received, and wherein ye stand; [2]by which also ye are saved, if ye keep in memory what I preached unto you, unless ye have believed in vain.

[3]For I delivered unto you first of all that which I also received, how that Christ died for our sins according to the scriptures; [4]and that he was buried, and that he rose again the third day according to the scriptures: [5]and that he was seen of Cephas, then of the twelve: [6]after that, he was seen of above five hundred brethren at once; of whom the greater part remain unto this present, but some are fallen asleep. [7]After that, he was seen of James; then of all the apostles. [8]And last of all he was seen of me also, as of one born out of due time.

[9]For I am the least of the apostles, that am not meet to be called an apostle, because I persecuted the church of God. [10]But by the grace of God I am what I am: and his grace which was bestowed upon me was not in vain; but I laboured more abundantly than they all: yet not I, but the grace of God which was with me. [11]Therefore whether it were I or they, so we preach, and so ye believed.

[12]Now if Christ be preached that he rose from the dead, how say some among you that there is no resurrection of the dead? [13]But if there be no resurrection of the dead, then is Christ not risen: [14]and if Christ be not risen, then is our preaching vain, and your faith is also vain. [15]Yea, and we are found false witnesses of God; because we have testified

THE RESURRECTION OF CHRIST *by Bartoleme Esteban Murillo*

of God that he raised up Christ: whom he raised not up, if so be that the dead rise not. [16]For if the dead rise not, then is not Christ raised; [17]and if Christ be not raised, your faith is in vain; ye are yet in your sins. [18]Then they also which are fallen asleep in Christ are perished. [19]If in this life only we have hope in Christ, we are of all men most miserable.

Chapter 15

[20]But now is Christ risen from the dead, and become the firstfruits of them that slept. [21]For since by man came death, by man came also the resurrection of the dead. [22]For as in Adam all die, even so in Christ shall all be made alive. [23]But every man in his own order: Christ the firstfruits; afterward they that are Christ's at his coming. [24]Then cometh the end, when he shall have delivered up the kingdom to God, even the Father; when he shall have put down all rule and all authority and power. [25]For he must reign, till he hath put all enemies under his feet. [26]The last enemy that shall be destroyed is death. [27]For he hath put all things under his feet. But when he saith all things are put under him, it is manifest that he is excepted, which did put all things under him. [28]And when all things shall be subdued unto him, then shall the Son also himself be subject unto him that put all things under him, that God may be all in all.

At the Last Trump

Chapter 15

BEHOLD, I SHEW YOU A MYSTERY; WE SHALL NOT all sleep, but we shall all be changed, [52]in a moment, in the twinkling of an eye, at the last trump: for the trumpet shall sound, and the dead shall be raised incorruptible, and we shall be changed. [53]For this corruptible must put on incorruption, and this mortal must put on immortality. [54]So when this corruptible shall have put on incorruption, and this mortal shall have put on immortality, then shall be brought to pass the saying that is written, "Death is swallowed up in victory."

[55]"O death, where is thy sting? O grave, where is thy victory?"

[56]The sting of death is sin; and the strength of sin is the law. [57]But thanks be to God, which giveth us the victory through our Lord Jesus Christ.

[58]Therefore, my beloved brethren, be ye stedfast, unmoveable, always abounding in the work of the Lord, forasmuch as ye know that your labour is not in vain in the Lord.

THE SECOND EPISTLE OF
PAUL THE APOSTLE TO

THE CORINTHIANS

The Ministry of Reconciliation

Chapter 5

Therefore if any man be in Christ, he is a new creature: old things are passed away; behold, all things are become new. [18]And all things are of God, who hath reconciled us to himself by Jesus Christ, and hath given to us the ministry of reconciliation; [19]to wit, that God was in Christ, reconciling the world unto himself, not imputing their trespasses unto them; and hath committed unto us the word of reconciliation. [20]Now then we are ambassadors for Christ, as though God did beseech you by us: we pray you in Christ's stead, be ye reconciled to God. [21]For he hath made him to be sin for us, who knew no sin; that we might be made the righteousness of God in him.

We then, as workers together with him, beseech you also that ye receive not the grace of God in vain. [2]For he saith, "I have heard thee in a time accepted, and in the day of salvation have I succoured thee": behold, now is the accepted time; behold, now is the day of salvation.

Chapter 6

Generosity Encouraged

Chapter 9

Every man according as he purposeth in his heart, so let him give; not grudgingly, or of necessity: for God loveth a cheerful giver. [8]And God is able to make all grace abound toward you; that ye, always having all sufficiency in all things, may abound to every good work: [9](as it is written, "He hath dispersed abroad: he hath given to the poor: his righteousness remaineth for ever." [10]Now he that ministereth seed to the sower both minister bread for your food, and multiply your seed sown, and increase the fruits of your righteousness;) [11]being enriched in every thing to all bountifulness, which causeth through us thanksgiving to God.

THE EPISTLE OF PAUL THE APOSTLE TO

THE GALATIANS

Justification by Faith

Chapter 2

WE WHO ARE JEWS BY NATURE, AND NOT "sinners" of the Gentiles, [16]knowing that a man is not justified by the works of the law, but by the faith of Jesus Christ, even we have believed in Jesus Christ, that we might be justified by the faith of Christ, and not by the works of the law: for by the works of the law shall no flesh be justified.

[17]But if, while we seek to be justified by Christ, we ourselves also are found sinners, is therefore Christ the minister of sin? God forbid. [18]For if I build again the things which I destroyed, I make myself a transgressor. [19]For I through the law am dead to the law, that I might live unto God. [20]I am crucified with Christ: nevertheless I live: yet not I, but Christ liveth in me: and the life which I now live in the flesh I live by the faith of the Son of God, who loved me, and gave himself for me. [21]I do not frustrate the grace of God: for if righteousness come by the law, then Christ is dead in vain.

Law and Faith

Is the law then against the promises of God? God forbid: for if there had been a law given which could have given life, verily righteousness should have been by the law. [22]But the scripture hath concluded all under sin, that the promise by faith of Jesus Christ might be given to them that believe.

Chapter 3

[23]But before faith came, we were kept under the law, shut up unto the faith which should afterwards be revealed. [24]Wherefore the law was our schoolmaster to bring us unto Christ, that we might be justified by faith. [25]But after that faith is come, we are no longer under a schoolmaster.

[26]For ye are all the children of God by faith in Christ Jesus. [27]For as many of you as have been baptized into Christ have put on Christ. [28]There is neither Jew nor Greek, there is neither bond nor free, there is neither male nor female: for ye are all one in Christ Jesus. [29]And if ye be Christ's, then are ye Abraham's seed, and heirs according to the promise.

Now I say, That the heir, as long as he is a child, differeth nothing from a servant, though he be lord of all; [2]but is under tutors and governors until the time appointed of the father. [3]Even so we, when we were children, were in bondage under the elements of the world: [4]but when the fulness of the time was come, God sent forth his Son, made of a woman, made under the law, [5]to redeem them that were under the law, that we might receive the adoption of sons. [6]And because ye are sons, God hath sent forth the Spirit of his Son into your hearts, crying, "Abba, Father." [7]Wherefore thou art no more a servant, but a son; and if a son, then an heir of God through Christ.

Chapter 4

The Fruits of the Spirit

Chapter 5

FOR, BRETHREN, YE HAVE BEEN CALLED UNTO liberty; only use not liberty for an occasion to the flesh, but by love serve one another. [14]For all the law is fulfilled in one word, even in this; "Thou shalt love thy neighbour as thyself." [15]But if ye bite and devour one another, take heed that ye be not consumed one of another.

[16]This I say then, walk in the Spirit, and ye shall not fulfil the lust of the flesh. [17]For the flesh lusteth against the Spirit, and the Spirit against the flesh: and these are contrary the one to the other: so that ye cannot do the things that ye would. [18]But if ye be led of the Spirit, ye are not under the law.

[19]Now the works of the flesh are manifest, which are these; adultery, fornication, uncleanness, lasciviousness, [20]idolatry, witchcraft, hatred, variance, emulations, wrath, strife, seditions, heresies, [21]envyings, murders,

Pallas Expelling the Vices from the Garden of Virtue
by Andrea Mantegna

drunkenness, revellings, and such like: of the which I tell you before, as I have also told you in time past, that they which do such things shall not inherit the kingdom of God.

[22]But the fruit of the Spirit is love, joy, peace, long-suffering, gentleness, goodness, faith, [23]meekness, temperance: against such there is no law. [24]And they that are Christ's have crucified the flesh with the affections and lusts. [25]If we live in the Spirit, let us also walk in the Spirit.

Centre panel from TRYPTYCH REPRESENTING JUSTICE *by Jacobello del Fiore*

THE EPISTLE OF PAUL THE APOSTLE TO

THE
EPHESIANS

The Riches of Christ's Glory

Chapter 1

BLESSED BE THE GOD AND FATHER OF OUR LORD Jesus Christ, who hath blessed us with all spiritual blessings in heavenly places in Christ: [4]according as he hath chosen us in him before the foundation of the world, that we should be holy and without blame before him in love: [5]having predestinated us into the adoption of children by Jesus Christ to himself, according to the good pleasure of his will, [6]to the praise of the glory of his grace, wherein he hath made us accepted in the beloved. [7]In whom we have redemption through his blood, the forgiveness of sins, according to the riches of his grace; [8]wherein he hath abounded toward us in all wisdom and prudence; [9]having made known unto us the mystery of his will, according to his good pleasure which he hath purposed in himself: [10]that in the dispensation of the fulness of times he might gather together in one all things in Christ, both which are in heaven, and which are on earth; even in him: [11]in whom also we have obtained an in-

Chapter 1

heritance, being predestinated according to the purpose of him who worketh all things after the counsel of his own will: [12]that we should be to the praise of his glory, who first trusted in Christ.

[13]In whom ye also trusted, after that ye heard the word of truth, the gospel of your salvation: in whom also after that ye believed, ye were sealed with that holy Spirit of promise, [14]which is the earnest of our inheritance until the redemption of the purchased possession, unto the praise of his glory.

[15]Wherefore I also, after I heard of your faith in the Lord Jesus, and love unto all the saints, [16]cease not to give thanks for you, making mention of you in my prayers; [17]that the God of our Lord Jesus Christ, the Father of glory, may give unto you the spirit of wisdom and revelation in the knowledge of him: [18]the eyes of your understanding being enlightened; that ye may know what is the hope of his calling, and what the riches of the glory of his inheritance in the saints, [19]and what is the exceeding greatness of his power to us-ward who believe, according to the working of his mighty power, [20]which he wrought in Christ, when he raised him from the dead, and set him at his own right hand in the heavenly places, [21]far above all principality, and power, and might, and dominion, and every name that is named, not only in this world, but also in that which is to come: [22]and hath put all things under his feet, and gave him to be the head over all things to the church, [23]which is his body, the fulness of him that filleth all in all.

Paul's Prayer for the Ephesians

Chapter 3

FOR THIS CAUSE I BOW MY KNEES UNTO THE FATHER of our Lord Jesus Christ, [15]of whom the whole family in heaven and earth is named, [16]that he would grant you, according to the riches of his glory, to be strengthened with might by his Spirit in the inner man; [17]that Christ may dwell in your hearts by

THE VIRGIN ENTHRONED *by Pietro Perugino*

Chapter 3

faith; that ye, being rooted and grounded in love, [18]may be able to comprehend with all saints what is the breadth, and length and depth, and height; [19]and to know the love of Christ, which passeth knowledge, that ye might be filled with all the fulness of God.

[20]Now unto him that is able to do exceeding abundantly above all that we ask or think, according to the power that worketh in us, [21]unto him be glory in the church by Christ Jesus throughout all ages, world without end. Amen.

The Armour of God

Chapter 6

FINALLY, MY BRETHREN, BE STRONG IN THE LORD, and in the power of his might. [11]Put on the whole armour of God, that ye may be able to stand against the wiles of the devil. [12]For we wrestle not against flesh and blood, but against principalities, against powers, against the rulers of the darkness of this world, against spiritual wickedness in high places. [13]Wherefore take unto you the whole armour of God, that ye may be able to withstand in the evil day, and having done all, to stand. [14]Stand therefore, having your loins girt about with truth, and having on the breastplate of righteousness; [15]and your feet shod with the preparation of the gospel of peace; [16]above all, taking the shield of faith, wherewith ye shall be able to quench all the fiery darts of the wicked. [17]And take the helmet of salvation, and the sword of the Spirit, which is the word of God: [18]praying always with all prayer and supplication in the Spirit, and watching thereunto with all perseverance and supplication for all saints; [19]and for me, that utterance may be given unto me, that I may open my mouth boldly, to make known the mystery of the gospel [20]for which I am an ambassador in bonds: that therein I may speak boldly, as I ought to speak.

THE EPISTLE OF PAUL THE APOSTLE TO

THE PHILIPPIANS

The Example of Christ

Chapter 1

LET NOTHING BE DONE THROUGH STRIFE OR VAIN-glory; but in lowliness of mind let each esteem other better than themselves. [4]Look not every man on his own things, but every man also on the things of others. [5]Let this mind be in you, which was also in Christ Jesus:

[6]Who, being in the form of God,
Thought it not robbery to be equal with God:
[7]But made himself of no reputation,
And took upon him the form of a servant,
And was made in the likeness of men:
[8]And being found in fashion as a man,
He humbled himself
And became obedient unto death,
Even the death of the cross.
[9]Wherefore God also hath highly exalted him,
And given him a name which is above every name:

CHRIST BLESSING *by Giovanni Bellini*

[10]That at the name of Jesus every knee should bow,
Of things in heaven, and things in earth, and things under the earth;
[11]And that every tongue should confess that Jesus Christ is Lord,
To the glory of God the Father.

[12]Wherefore, my beloved, as ye have always obeyed, not as in my presence only, but now much more in my absence, work out your own salvation with fear and trembling. [13]For

Chapter 2

it is God which worketh in you both to will and to do of his good pleasure.

[14]Do all things without murmurings and disputings: [15]that ye may be blameless and harmless, the sons of God, without rebuke, in the midst of a crooked and perverse nation, among whom ye shine as lights in the world; [16]holding forth the word of life; that I may rejoice in the day of Christ, that I have not run in vain, neither laboured in vain.

Paul's Loss for Christ

Chapter 3

Finally, my brethren, rejoice in the Lord. To write the same things to you, to me indeed is not grievous, but for you it is safe.

[2]Beware of dogs, beware of evil workers, beware of the concision. [3]For we are the circumcision, which worship God in the spirit, and rejoice in Christ Jesus, and have no confidence in the flesh. [4]Though I might also have confidence in the flesh.

If any other man thinketh that he hath whereof he might trust in the flesh, I more: [5]circumcised the eighth day, of the stock of Israel, of the tribe of Benjamin, an Hebrew of the Hebrews; as touching the law, a Pharisee; [6]concerning zeal, persecuting the church; touching the righteousness which is in the law, blameless.

[7]But what things were gain to me, those I counted loss for Christ. [8]Yea doubtless, and I count all things but loss for the excellency of the knowledge of Christ Jesus my Lord: for whom I have suffered the loss of all things, and do count them but dung, that I may win Christ, [9]and be found in him, not having mine own righteousness, which is of the law, but that which is through the faith of Christ, the righteousness which is of God by faith: [10]that I may know him, and the power of his resurrection, and the fellowship of his sufferings, being made conformable unto his death; [11]if by any means I might attain unto the resurrection of the dead.

[12]Not as though I had already attained, either were already perfect: but I follow after, if that I may apprehend

Chapter 3

that for which also I am apprehended of Christ Jesus. [13]Brethren, I count not myself to have apprehended: but this one thing I do, forgetting those things which are behind, and reaching forth unto those things which are before, [14]I press toward the mark for the prize of the high calling of God in Christ Jesus.

[15]Let us therefore, as many as be perfect, be thus minded: and if in any thing ye be otherwise minded, God shall reveal even this unto you. [16]Nevertheless, whereto we have already attained, let us walk by the same rule, let us mind the same thing.

"Rejoice in the Lord"

Chapter 4

Rejoice in the Lord alway: and again I say, rejoice. [5]Let your moderation be known unto all men. The Lord is at hand. [6]Be careful for nothing; but in every thing by prayer and supplication with thanksgiving let your requests be made known unto God. [7]And the peace of God, which passeth all understanding, shall keep your hearts and minds through Christ Jesus.

[8]Finally, brethren, whatsoever things are true, whatoever things are honest, whatsoever things are just, whatsoever things are pure, whatsoever things are lovely, whatsoever things are of good report; if there be any virtue, and if there be any praise, think on these things. [9]Those things, which ye have both learned, and received, and heard, and seen in me, do: and the God of peace shall be with you.

[10]But I rejoiced in the Lord greatly, that now at the last your care of me hath flourished again; wherein ye were also careful, but ye lacked opportunity. [11]Not that I speak in respect of want: for I have learned, in whatsoever state I am, therewith to be content. [12]I know both how to be abased, and I know how to abound: everywhere and in all things I am instructed both to be full and to be hungry, both to abound and to suffer need. [13]I can do all things through Christ which strengtheneth me.

THE EPISTLE OF PAUL THE APOSTLE TO

THE COLOSSIANS

Paul's Prayer for the Colossians

Chapter 1

WE GIVE THANKS TO GOD AND THE FATHER of our Lord Jesus Christ, praying always for you, [4]since we heard of your faith in Christ Jesus, and of the love which ye have to all the saints, [5]for the hope which is laid up for you in heaven, whereof ye heard before in the word of the truth of the gospel; [6]which is come unto you, as it is in all the world; and bringeth forth fruit, as it doth also in you, since the day ye heard of it, and knew the grace of God in truth: [7]as ye also learned of Epaphras our dear fellowservant, who is for you a faithful minister of Christ; [8]who also declared unto us your love in the Spirit.

[9]For this cause we also, since the day we heard it, do not cease to pray for you, and to desire that ye might be filled with the knowledge of his will in all wisdom and spiritual understanding; [10]that ye might walk worthy of the Lord unto all pleasing, being fruitful in every good work, and increasing in the knowledge of God; [11]strengthened with all

Chapter 1

might, according to his glorious power, unto all patience and longsuffering with joyfulness; [12]giving thanks unto the Father, which hath made us meet to be partakers of the inheritance of the saints in light: [13]who hath delivered us from the power of darkness, and hath translated us into the kingdom of his dear Son: [14]in whom we have redemption through his blood, even the forgiveness of sins: [15]who is the image of the invisible God, the firstborn of every creature: [16]for by him were all things created, that are in heaven, and that are in earth, visible and invisible, whether they be thrones, or dominions, or principalities, or powers: all things were created by him, and for him: [17]and he is before all things, and by him all things consist.

[18]And he is the head of the body, the church: who is the beginning, the firstborn from the dead; that in all things he might have the preeminence. [19]For it pleased the Father that in him should all fulness dwell; [20]and, having made peace through the blood of his cross, by him to reconcile all things unto himself; by him, I say, whether they be things in earth, or things in heaven.

Risen With Christ

Chapter 3

IF YE THEN BE RISEN WITH CHRIST, SEEK THOSE THINGS which are above, where Christ sitteth on the right hand of God. [2]Set your affection on things above, not on things on the earth. [3]For ye are dead, and your life is hid with Christ in God. [4]When Christ, who is our life, shall appear, then shall ye also appear with him in glory.

[5]Mortify therefore your members which are upon the earth; fornication, uncleanness, inordinate affection, evil concupiscence, and covetousness, which is idolatry: [6]for which things' sake the wrath of God cometh on the children of disobedience: [7]in the which ye also walked some time, when ye lived in them. [8]But now ye also put off all these; anger, wrath, malice, blasphemy, filthy communication out of your mouth. [9]Lie not one to another, seeing

THE CHOSEN ARE CALLED TO HEAVEN *by Luca Signorelli*

that ye have put off the old man with his deeds; [10]and have put on the new man, which is renewed in knowledge after the image of him that created him: [11]where there is neither Greek nor Jew, circumcision nor uncircumcision, Barbarian, Scythian, bond nor free: but Christ is all, and in all.

[12]Put on therefore, as the elect of God, holy and beloved, bowels of mercies, kindness, humbleness of mind, meekness, longsuffering; [13]forbearing one another, and forgiving one another, if any man have a quarrel against any: even as Christ forgave you, so also do ye. [14]And above all these things put on charity, which is the bond of perfectness.

[15]And let the peace of God rule in your hearts, to the which also ye are called in one body; and be ye thankful. [16]Let the word of Christ dwell in you richly in all wisdom; teaching and admonishing one another in psalms and hymns and spiritual songs, singing with grace in your hearts to the Lord. [17]And whatsoever ye do in word or deed, do all in the name of the Lord Jesus, giving thanks to God and the Father by him.

THE FIRST EPISTLE OF
PAUL THE APOSTLE TO

THE THESSALONIANS

The Coming of the Lord

Chapter 4

But I would not have you to be ignorant, brethren, concerning them which are asleep, that ye sorrow not, even as others which have no hope. [14]For if we believe that Jesus died and rose again, even so them also which sleep in Jesus will God bring with him. [15]For this we say unto you by the word of the Lord, that we which are alive and remain unto the coming of the Lord shall not prevent them which are asleep. [16]For the Lord himself shall descend from heaven with a shout, with the voice of the archangel, and with the trump of God: and the dead in Christ shall rise first: [17]then we which are alive and remain shall be caught up together with them in the clouds, to meet the Lord in the air: and so shall we ever be with the Lord. [18]Wherefore comfort one another with these words.

Chapter 5

BUT OF THE TIMES AND THE SEASONS, BRETHREN, YE HAVE no need that I write unto you. [2]For yourselves know perfectly that the day of the Lord so cometh as a thief in the night. [3]For when they shall say, "Peace and safety"; then sudden destruction cometh upon them, as travail upon a woman with child; and they shall not escape.

[4]But ye, brethren, are not in darkness, that that day should overtake you as a thief. [5]Ye are all the children of light, and the children of the day: we are not of the night, nor of darkness. [6]Therefore let us not sleep, as do others; but let us watch and be sober. [7]For they that sleep sleep in the night; and they that be drunken are drunken in the night. [8]But let us, who are of the day, be sober, putting on the breastplate of faith and love; and for an helmet, the hope of salvation. [9]For God hath not appointed us to wrath, but to obtain salvation by our Lord Jesus Christ, [10]who died for us, that, whether we wake or sleep, we should live together with him. [11]Wherefore comfort yourselves together, and edify one another, even as also ye do.

EXHORTATIONS TO HOLY LIVING

Chapter 5

NOW WE EXHORT YOU, BRETHREN, WARN THEM that are unruly, comfort the feebleminded, support the weak, be patient toward all men. [15]See that none render evil for evil unto any man; but ever follow that which is good, both among yourselves, and to all men.

[16]Rejoice evermore. [17]Pray without ceasing. [18]In every thing give thanks: for this is the will of God in Christ Jesus concerning you.

[19]Quench not the Spirit. [20]Despise not prophesyings. [21]Prove all things; hold fast that which is good. [22]Abstain from all appearance of evil.

[23]And the very God of peace sanctify you wholly; and I pray God your whole spirit and soul and body be preserved blameless unto the coming of our Lord Jesus Christ. [24]Faithful is he that calleth you, who also will do it.

THE FIRST EPISTLE OF
PAUL THE APOSTLE TO

TIMOTHY

The Lord's Mercy to Paul

Chapter 1

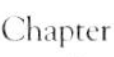

This is a faithful saying, and worthy of all acceptation, that Christ Jesus came into the world to save sinners; of whom I am chief. [16]Howbeit for this cause I obtained mercy, that in me first Jesus Christ might shew forth all longsuffering, for a pattern to them which should hereafter believe on him to life everlasting. [17]Now unto the King eternal, immortal, invisible, the only wise God, be honour and glory for ever and ever. Amen.

[18]This charge I commit unto thee, son Timothy, according to the prophecies which went before on thee, that thou by them mightest war a good warfare; [19]holding faith, and a good conscience; which some having put away concerning faith have made shipwreck: [20]of whom is Hymenaeus and Alexander; whom I have delivered unto Satan, that they may learn not to blaspheme.

Chapter 2

I EXHORT THEREFORE, THAT, FIRST OF ALL, SUPPLICATIONS, prayers, intercessions, and giving of thanks, be made for all men; [2]for kings, and for all that are in authority; that we may lead a quiet and peaceable life in all godliness and honesty. [3]For this is good and acceptable in the sight of God our Saviour; [4]who will have all men to be saved, and to come unto the knowledge of the truth. [5]For there is one God, and one mediator between God and men, the man Christ Jesus; [6]who gave himself a ransom for all, to be testified in due time. [7]Whereunto I am ordained a preacher, and an apostle, (I speak the truth in Christ, and lie not;) a teacher of the Gentiles in faith and verity.

The Love of Money

Chapter 6

IF ANY MAN TEACH OTHERWISE, AND CONSENT NOT TO wholesome words, even the words of our Lord Jesus Christ, and to the doctrine which is according to godliness; [4]he is proud, knowing nothing, but doting about questions and strifes of words, whereof cometh envy, strife, railings, evil surmisings, [5]perverse disputings of men of corrupt minds, and destitute of the truth, supposing that gain is godliness: from such withdraw thyself.

[6]But godliness with contentment is great gain. [7]For we brought nothing into this world, and it is certain we can carry nothing out. [8]And having food and raiment let us be therewith content. [9]But they that will be rich fall into temptation and a snare, and into many foolish and hurtful lusts, which drown men in destruction and perdition. [10]For the love of money is the root of all evil: which while some coveted after, they have erred from the faith, and pierced themselves through with many sorrows.

[11]But thou, O man of God, flee these things; and follow after righteousness, godliness, faith, love, patience, meekness. [12]Fight the good fight of faith, lay hold on eternal life, whereunto thou art also called, and hast professed a good profession before many witnesses. [13]I give thee charge in the sight of God, who quickeneth all things, and before

Detail from AN ALLEGORY OF TEMPERANCE AND EXCESS, *Anglo-Netherlands School*

Christ Jesus, who before Pontius Pilate witnessed a good confession; [14]that thou keep this commandment without spot, unrebukeable, until the appearing of our Lord Jesus Christ: [15]which in his times he shall shew, who is the blessed and only Potentate, the King of kings, and Lord of lords; [16]who only hath immortality, dwelling in the light which no man can approach unto; whom no man hath seen, nor can see: to whom be honour and power everlasting. Amen.

[17]Charge them that are rich in this world, that they be not highminded, nor trust in uncertain riches, but in the living God, who giveth us richly all things to enjoy; [18]that they do good, that they be rich in good works, ready to distribute, willing to communicate; [19]laying up in store for themselves a good foundation against the time to come, that they may lay hold on eternal life.

THE SECOND EPISTLE OF
PAUL THE APOSTLE TO

TIMOTHY

The Soldier of Christ

Chapter 2

THOU THEREFORE, MY SON, BE STRONG IN THE grace that is in Christ Jesus. [2]And the things that thou hast heard of me among many witnesses, the same commit thou to faithful men, who shall be able to teach others also. [3]Thou therefore endure hardness, as a good soldier of Jesus Christ. [4]No man that warreth entangleth himself with the affairs of this life; that he may please him who hath chosen him to be a soldier. [5]And if a man also strive for masteries, yet is he not crowned, except he strive lawfully. [6]The husbandman that laboureth must be first partaker of the fruits. [7]Consider what I say; and the Lord give thee understanding in all things.

[8]Remember that Jesus Christ of the seed of David was raised from the dead according to my gospel: [9]wherein I suffer trouble, as an evil doer, even unto bonds; but the word of God is not bound. [10]Therefore I endure all things for the elect's sakes, that they may also obtain the salvation which is in Christ Jesus with eternal glory.

[11]It is a faithful saying:

For if we be dead with him,
We shall also live with him:
[12] If we suffer,
We shall also reign with him:
If we deny him,
He also will deny us:
[13]If we believe not,
Yet he abideth faithful:
He cannot deny himself.

Left panel from the Ghent Altarpiece *by Jan van Eyck*

Paul's Charge to Timothy

Chapter 3

BUT CONTINUE THOU IN THE THINGS WHICH thou hast learned and hast been assured of, knowing of whom thou hast learned them; [15]and that from a child thou hast known the holy scriptures, which are able to make thee wise unto salvation through faith which is in Christ Jesus. [16]All scripture is given by inspiration of God, and is profitable for doctrine, for reproof, for correction, for instruction in righteousness: [17]that the man of God may be perfect, throughly furnished unto all good works.

Chapter 4

I CHARGE THEE THEREFORE BEFORE GOD, AND THE LORD Jesus Christ, who shall judge the quick and the dead at his appearing and his kingdom; [2]preach the word; be instant in season, out of season; reprove, rebuke, exhort with all longsuffering and doctrine. [3]For the time will come when they will not endure sound doctrine; but after their own lusts shall they heap to themselves teachers, having itching ears; [4]and they shall turn away their ears from the truth, and shall be turned unto fables. [5]But watch thou in all things, endure afflictions, do the work of an evangelist, make full proof of thy ministry.

[6]For I am now ready to be offered, and the time of my departure is at hand. [7]I have fought a good fight, I have finished my course, I have kept the faith: [8]henceforth there is laid up for me a crown of righteousness, which the Lord, the righteous judge, shall give me at that day: and not to me only, but unto all them also that love his appearing.

THE EPISTLE OF PAUL THE APOSTLE TO

THE
HEBREWS

The Son Superior to Angels

Chapter 1

GOD, WHO AT SUNDRY TIMES AND IN DIVERS manners spake in time past unto the fathers by the prophets, [2]hath in these last days spoken unto us by his Son, whom he hath appointed heir of all things, by whom also he made the worlds; [3]who being the brightness of his glory, and the express image of his person, and upholding all things by the word of his power, when he had by himself purged our sins, sat down on the right hand of the Majesty on high; [4]being made so much better than the angels, as he hath by inheritance obtained a more excellent name than they.

Jesus Greater Than Moses

Chapter 3

WHEREFORE, HOLY BRETHREN, PARTAKERS of the heavenly calling, consider the Apostle and High Priest of our profession, Christ Jesus; [2]who was faithful to him that appointed him, as also Moses was faithful in all his house. [3]For this man was counted worthy of more glory than Moses, inasmuch as he who hath

Allegory of the Old and New Testaments *by Hans Holbein the Younger*

Chapter 3

builded the house hath more honour than the house. [4]For every house is builded by some man; but he that built all things is God. [5]And Moses verily was faithful in all his house, as a servant, for a testimony of those things which were to be spoken after; [6]but Christ as a son over his own house; whose house are we, if we hold fast the confidence and the rejoicing of the hope firm unto the end.

Jesus the Great High Priest

Chapter 4

SEEING THEN THAT WE HAVE A GREAT HIGH priest, that is passed into the heavens, Jesus the Son of God, let us hold fast our profession. [15]For we have not an high priest which cannot be touched with the feeling of our infirmities; but was in all points tempted like as we are, yet without sin. [16]Let us therefore come boldly unto the throne of grace, that we may obtain mercy, and find grace to help in time of need.

Examples of Faith

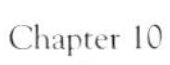

Chapter 10

CAST NOT AWAY THEREFORE YOUR CONFIDENCE, which hath great recompence of reward. [36]For ye have need of patience, that, after ye have done the will of God, ye might receive the promise. [37]For yet a little while, and "He that shall come will come, and will not tarry. [38]Now the just shall live by faith: but if any man draw back, my soul shall have no pleasure in him." [39]But we are not of them who draw back unto perdition; but of them that believe to the saving of the soul.

Chapter 11

NOW FAITH IS THE SUBSTANCE OF THINGS HOPED FOR, THE evidence of things not seen. [2]For by it the elders obtained a good report.

[3]Through faith we understand that the worlds were framed by the word of God, so that things which are seen were not made of things which do appear.

[4]By faith Abel offered unto God a more excellent sacrifice than Cain, by which he obtained witness that he was righteous, God testifying of his gifts: and by it he being dead yet speaketh.

[5]By faith Enoch was translated that he should not see death; and was not found, because God had translated him: for before his translation he had this testimony, that he pleased God. [6]But without faith it is impossible to please him: for he that cometh to God must believe that he is, and that he is a rewarder of them that diligently seek him.

[7]By faith Noah, being warned of God of things not seen as yet, moved with fear, prepared an ark to the saving of his house; by the which he condemned the world, and became heir of the righteousness which is by faith.

[8]By faith Abraham, when he was called to go out into a place which he should after receive for an inheritance, obeyed; and he went out, not knowing whither he went. [9]By faith he sojourned in the land of promise, as in a strange country, dwelling in tabernacles with Isaac and Jacob, the heirs with him of the same promise: [10]for he looked for a city which hath foundations, whose builder and maker is God.

[11]Through faith also Sarah herself received strength to conceive seed, and was delivered of a child when she was past age, because she judged him faithful who had promised. [12]Therefore sprang there even of one, and him as good as dead, so many as the stars of the sky in multitude, and as the sand which is by the sea shore innumerable.

[13]These all died in faith, not having received the promises, but having seen them afar off, and were persuaded of them, and embraced them, and confessed that they were strangers and pilgrims on the earth. [14]For they that say such things declare plainly that they seek a country. [15]And truly, if they had been mindful of that country from whence they came out, they might have had opportunity to have returned. [16]But now they desire a better country, that is, an heavenly: wherefore God is not ashamed to be called their God: for he hath prepared for them a city.

[17]By faith Abraham, when he was tried, offered up Isaac: and he that had received the promises offered up his only begotten son, [18]of whom it was said, that "In Isaac shall thy seed be called": [19]accounting that God was able to raise him up, even from the dead; from whence also he received him in a figure.

[20]By faith Isaac blessed Jacob and Esau concerning things to come.

[21]By faith Jacob, when he was a dying, blessed both the sons of Joseph; and worshipped, leaning upon the top of his staff.

[22]By faith, Joseph, when he died, made mention of the departing of the children of Israel; and gave commandment concerning his bones.

[23]By faith Moses, when he was born, was hid three months of his parents, because they saw he was a proper child; and they were not afraid of the king's commandment.

[24]By faith Moses, when he was come to years, refused to be called the son of Pharaoh's daughter; [25]choosing rather to suffer affliction with the people of God, than to enjoy the pleasures of sin for a season; [26]esteeming the reproach of Christ greater riches than the treasures in Egypt: for he had respect unto the recompence of the reward. [27]By faith he forsook Egypt, not fearing the wrath of the king: for he endured, as seeing him who is invisible. [28]Through faith he kept the passover, and the sprinkling of blood, lest he that destroyed the firstborn should touch them.

[29]By faith they passed through the Red sea as by dry land: which the Egyptians assaying to do were drowned.

[30]By faith the walls of Jericho fell down, after they were compassed about seven days.

[31]By faith the harlot Rahab perished not with them that believed not, when she had received the spies with peace.

[32]And what shall I more say? For the time would fail me to tell of Gedeon, and of Barak, and of Samson, and of Jephthae; of David also, and Samuel, and of the prophets: [33]who through faith subdued kingdoms, wrought righteousness, obtained promises, stopped the mouths of lions, [34]quenched the violence of fire, escaped the edge of the sword, out of weakness were made strong, waxed valiant in fight, turned to flight the armies of the aliens. [35]Women received their dead raised to life again: and others were tortured, not accepting deliverance; that they might obtain a better resurrection: [36]and others had trial of cruel mockings and scourgings, yea, moreover of bonds and imprisonment: [37]they were stoned, they were sawn asunder, were tempted, were slain with the sword: they wandered about in sheep-

Chapter 12

skins and goatskins; being destitute, afflicted, tormented; [38](of whom the world was not worthy:) they wandered in deserts, and in mountains, and in dens and caves of the earth.

[39]And these all, having obtained a good report through faith, received not the promise: [40]God having provided some better thing for us, that they without us should not be made perfect.

The Example of Jesus

Chapter 12

WHEREFORE SEEING WE ALSO ARE COMpassed about with so great a cloud of witnesses, let us lay aside every weight, and the sin which doth so easily beset us, and let us run with patience the race that is set before us, [2]looking unto Jesus the author and finisher of our faith; who for the joy that was set before him endured the cross, despising the shame, and is set down at the right hand of the throne of God. [3]For consider him that endured such contradiction of sinners against himself, lest ye be wearied and faint in your minds.

The Heavenly Jerusalem

Chapter 12

FOR YE ARE NOT COME UNTO THE MOUNT THAT might be touched, and that burned with fire, nor unto blackness, and darkness, and tempest, [19]and the sound of a trumpet, and the voice of words; which voice they that heard entreated that the word should not be spoken to them any more: [20](for they could not endure that which was commanded, "And if so much as a beast touch the mountain, it shall be stoned, or thrust through with a dart: [21]and so terrible was the sight, that Moses said, "I exceedingly fear and quake":) [22]but ye

Adoration of the Trinity *by Albrecht Dürer*

are come unto mount Sion, and unto the city of the living God, the heavenly Jerusalem, and to an innumerable company of angels, [23]to the general assembly and church of the firstborn, which are written in heaven, and to God the Judge of all, and to the spirits of just men made perfect, [24]and to Jesus the mediator of the new covenant, and to the blood of sprinkling, that speaketh better things than that of Abel.

Chapter 12

Love and Contentment

Chapter 13

LET BROTHERLY LOVE CONTINUE. [2]BE NOT FORGETful to entertain strangers: for thereby some have entertained angels unawares. [3]Remember them that are in bonds, as bound with them; and them which suffer adversity, as being yourselves also in the body.

[4]Marriage is honourable in all, and the bed undefiled: but whoremongers and adulterers God will judge. [5]Let your conversation be without covetousness; and be content with such things as ye have: for he hath said, "I will never leave thee, nor forsake thee." [6]So that we may boldly say, "The Lord is my helper, and I will not fear what men shall do unto me."

[7]Remember them which have the rule over you, who have spoken unto you the word of God: whose faith follow, considering the end of their conversation. [8]Jesus Christ the same yesterday, and to day, and for ever.

A Prayer for the Hebrews

Chapter 13

NOW THE GOD OF PEACE, THAT BROUGHT again from the dead our Lord Jesus, that great shepherd of the sheep, through the blood of the everlasting covenant, [21]make you perfect in every good work to do his will, working in you that which is wellpleasing in his sight, through Jesus Christ; to whom be glory for ever and ever. Amen.

THE GENERAL EPISTLE OF

JAMES

Hearing and Doing

Chapter 1

EVERY GOOD GIFT AND EVERY PERFECT GIFT IS FROM above, and cometh down from the Father of lights, with whom is no variableness, neither shadow of turning. [18]Of his own will begat he us with the word of truth, that we should be a kind of firstfruits of his creatures.

[19]Wherefore, my beloved brethren, let every man be swift to hear, slow to speak, slow to wrath: [20]for the wrath of man worketh not the righteousness of God. [21]Wherefore lay apart all filthiness and superfluity of naughtiness, and receive with meekness the engrafted word, which is able to save your souls.

[22]But be ye doers of the word, and not hearers only, deceiving your own selves. [23]For if any be a hearer of the word, and not a doer, he is like unto a man beholding his natural face in a glass: [24]for he beholdeth himself, and goeth his way, and straightway forgetteth what manner of man he was. [25]But whoso looketh into the perfect law of

Chapter 1

liberty, and continueth therein, he being not a forgetful hearer, but a doer of the work, this man shall be blessed in his deed.

[26]If any man among you seem to be religious, and bridleth not his tongue, but deceiveth his own heart, this man's religion is vain. [27]Pure religion and undefiled before God and the Father is this, to visit the fatherless and widows in their affliction, and to keep himself unspotted from the world.

Faith and Works

Chapter 2

WHAT DOTH IT PROFIT, MY BRETHREN, though a man say he hath faith, and have not works? Can faith save him? [15]If a brother or sister be naked, and destitute of daily food, [16]and one of you say unto them, "Depart in peace, be ye warmed and filled"; notwithstanding ye give them not those things which are needful to the body; what doth it profit? [17]Even so faith, if it hath not works, is dead, being alone.

[18]Yea, a man may say, "Thou hast faith, and I have works": shew me thy faith without thy works, and I will shew thee my faith by my works. [19]Thou believest that there is one God; thou doest well: the devils also believe, and tremble.

[20]But wilt thou know, O vain man, that faith without works is dead? [21]Was not Abraham our father justified by works, when he had offered Isaac his son upon the altar? [22]Seest thou how faith wrought with his works, and by works was faith made perfect? [23]And the scripture was fulfilled which saith, "Abraham believed God, and it was imputed unto him for righteousness": and he was called the Friend of God. [24]Ye see then how that by works a man is justified, and not by faith only.

[25]Likewise also was not Rahab the harlot justified by works, when she had received the messengers, and had sent them out another way? [26]For as the body without the spirit is dead, so faith without works is dead also.

INDUSTRY TRIUMPHING OVER LAZINESS *by Giovanni-Battista Tiepolo*

THE FIRST EPISTLE GENERAL OF

PETER

A Lively Hope

Chapter 1

BLESSED BE THE GOD AND FATHER OF OUR LORD Jesus Christ, which according to his abundant mercy hath begotten us again unto a lively hope by the resurrection of Jesus Christ from the dead, [4]to an inheritance incorruptible, and undefiled, and that fadeth not away, reserved in heaven for you, [5]who are kept by the power of God through faith unto salvation ready to be revealed in the last time. [6]Wherein ye greatly rejoice, though now for a season, if need be, ye are in heaviness through manifold temptations: [7]that the trial of your faith, being much more precious than of gold that perisheth, though it be tried with fire, might be found unto praise and honour and glory at the appearing of Jesus Christ: [8]whom having not seen, ye love; in whom, though now ye see him not, yet believing, ye rejoice with joy unspeakable and full of glory: [9]receiving the end of your faith, even the salvation of your souls.

A Chosen People

Chapter 2

WHEREFORE LAYING ASIDE ALL MALICE, and all guile, and hypocrisies, and envies, and all evil speakings, [2]as newborn babes, desire the sincere milk of the word, that ye may grow thereby: [3]if so be ye have tasted that the Lord is gracious.

[4]To whom coming, as unto a living stone, disallowed indeed of men, but chosen of God, and precious, [5]ye also, as lively stones, are built up a spiritual house, an holy priesthood, to offer up spiritual sacrifices, acceptable to God by Jesus Christ. [6]Wherefore also it is contained in the scripture, "Behold, I lay in Sion a chief corner stone, elect, precious: and he that believeth on him shall not be confounded." [7]Unto you therefore which believe he is precious: but unto them which be disobedient, "The stone which the builders disallowed, the same is made the head of the corner", [8]and "a stone of stumbling, and a rock of offence", even to them which stumble at the word, being disobedient: whereunto also they were appointed.

DISPUTA *by Raphael*

Chapter 2

[9]But ye are a chosen generation, a royal priesthood, an holy nation, a peculiar people; that ye should shew forth the praises of him who hath called you out of darkness into his marvellous light: [10]which in time past were not a people, but are now the people of God: which had not obtained mercy, but now have obtained mercy.

Good Stewardship

Chapter 4

But the end of all things is at hand: be ye therefore sober, and watch unto prayer. [8]And above all things have fervent charity among yourselves: for charity shall cover the multitude of sins. [9]Use hospitality one to another without grudging. [10]As every man hath received the gift, even so minister the same one to another, as good stewards of the manifold grace of God. [11]If any man speak, let him speak as the oracles of God; if any man minister, let him do it as of the ability which God giveth: that God in all things may be glorified through Jesus Christ, to whom be praise and dominion for ever and ever. Amen.

THE SECOND EPISTLE GENERAL OF

PETER

Peter's Testimony

Chapter 1

SIMON PETER, A SERVANT AND AN APOSTLE OF Jesus Christ, to them that have obtained like precious faith with us through the righteousness of God and our Saviour Jesus Christ:

[2]Grace and peace be multiplied unto you through the knowledge of God, and of Jesus our Lord, [3]according as his divine power hath given unto us all things that pertain unto life and godliness, through the knowledge of him that hath called us to glory and virtue: [4]whereby are given unto us exceeding great and precious promises: that by these ye might be partakers of the divine nature, having escaped the corruption that is in the world through lust.

[5]And beside this, giving all diligence, add to your faith virtue; and to virtue knowledge; [6]and to knowledge temperance; and to temperance patience; and to patience godliness; [7]and to godliness brotherly kindness; and to brotherly kindness charity. [8]For if these things be in you, and

WISDOM *by Titian*

abound, they make you that ye shall neither be barren nor unfruitful in the knowledge of our Lord Jesus Christ. [9]But he that lacketh these things is blind, and cannot see afar off, and hath forgotten that he was purged from his old sins.

[10]Wherefore the rather, brethren, give diligence to make your calling and election sure: for if ye do these things, ye shall never fall: [11]for so an entrance shall be ministered unto you abundantly into the everlasting kingdom of our Lord and Saviour Jesus Christ.

[12]Wherefore I will not be negligent to put you always in remembrance of these things, though ye know them, and be established in the present truth. [13]Yea, I think it meet, as long as I am in this tabernacle, to stir you up by putting you in remembrance; [14]knowing that shortly I must put off this my tabernacle, even as our Lord Jesus Christ hath shewed me. [15]Moreover I will endeavour that ye may be able after my decease to have these things always in remembrance.

Chapter 1

[16]For we have not followed cunningly devised fables, when we made known unto you the power and coming of our Lord Jesus Christ, but were eyewitnesses of his majesty. [17]For he received from God the Father honour and glory, when there came such a voice to him from the excellent glory, "This is my beloved Son, in whom I am well pleased." [18]And this voice which came from heaven we heard, when we were with him in the holy mount.

[19]We have also a more sure word of prophecy; whereunto ye do well that ye take heed, as unto a light that shineth in a dark place, until the day dawn, and the day star arise in your hearts: [20]knowing this first, that no prophecy of the scripture is of any private interpretation. [21]For the prophecy came not in old time by the will of man: but holy men of God spake as they were moved by the Holy Ghost.

The Day of the Lord

Chapter 3

But, beloved, be not ignorant of this one thing, that one day is with the Lord as a thousand years, and a thousand years as one day. [9]The Lord is not slack concerning his promise, as some men count slackness; but is longsuffering to us-ward, not willing that any should perish, but that all should come to repentance.

[10]But the day of the Lord will come as a thief in the night; in the which the heavens shall pass away with a great noise, and the elements shall melt with fervent heat, the earth also and the works that are therein shall be burned up.

[11]Seeing then that all these things shall be dissolved, what manner of persons ought ye to be in all holy conversation and godliness, [12]looking for and hasting unto the coming of the day of God, wherein the heavens being on fire shall be dissolved, and the elements shall melt with fervent heat? [13]Nevertheless we, according to his promise, look for new heavens and a new earth, wherein dwelleth righteousness. [14]Wherefore, beloved, seeing that ye look for such things, be diligent that ye may be found of him in peace, without spot, and blameless.

THE FIRST EPISTLE GENERAL OF

JOHN

God is Light

Chapter 1

THAT WHICH WAS FROM THE BEGINNING, WHICH we have heard, which we have seen with our eyes, which we have looked upon, and our hands have handled, of the Word of life; [2](for the life was manifested, and we have seen it, and bear witness, and shew unto you that eternal life, which was with the Father, and was manifested unto us;) [3]that which we have seen and heard declare we unto you, that ye also may have fellowship with us: and truly our fellowship is with the Father, and with his Son Jesus Christ. [4]And these things write we unto you, that your joy may be full.

[5]This then is the message which we have heard of him, and declare unto you, that God is light, and in him is no darkness at all. [6]If we say that we have fellowship with him, and walk in darkness, we lie, and do not the truth: [7]but if we walk in the light, as he is in the light, we have fellow-

ship one with another, and the blood of Jesus Christ his Son cleanseth us from all sin.

[8]If we say that we have no sin, we deceive ourselves, and the truth is not in us. [9]If we confess our sins, he is faithful and just to forgive us our sins, and to cleanse us from all unrighteousness. [10]If we say that we have not sinned, we make him a liar, and his word is not in us.

The Holy Trinity *by Tiziano Titian*

Chapter 2

My little children, these things write I unto you, that ye sin not. And if any man sin, we have an advocate with the Father, Jesus Christ the righteous: 2and he is the propitiation for our sins: and not for ours only, but also for the sins of the whole world.

3And hereby we do know that we know him, if we keep his commandments. 4He that saith, "I know him," and keepeth not his commandments, is a liar, and the truth is not in him. 5But whoso keepeth his word, in him verily is the love of God perfected: hereby know we that we are in him. 6He that saith he abideth in him ought himself also so to walk, even as he walked.

7Brethren, I write no new commandment unto you, but an old commandment which ye had from the beginning. The old commandment is the word which ye have heard from the beginning. 8Again, a new commandment I write unto you, which thing is true in him and in you: because the darkness is past, and the true light now shineth.

9He that saith he is in the light, and hateth his brother, is in darkness even until now. 10He that loveth his brother abideth in the light, and there is none occasion of stumbling in him. 11But he that hateth his brother is in darkness, and walketh in darkness, and knoweth not whither he goeth, because that darkness hath blinded his eyes.

Sons of God

Chapter 3

Behold, what manner of love the Father hath bestowed upon us, that we should be called the sons of God: therefore the world knoweth us not, because it knew him not. 2Beloved, now are we the sons of God, and it doth not yet appear what we shall be: but we know that, when he shall appear, we shall be like him; for we shall see him as he is. 3And every man that hath this hope in him purifieth himself, even as he is pure.

Chapter 3

[4]Whosoever committeth sin transgresseth also the law: for sin is the transgression of the law. [5]And ye know that he was manifested to take away our sins; and in him is no sin. [6]Whosoever abideth in him sinneth not: whosoever sinneth hath not seen him, neither known him.

[7]Little children, let no man deceive you: he that doeth righteousness is righteous, even as he is righteous. [8]He that committeth sin is of the devil; for the devil sinneth from the beginning. For this purpose the Son of God was manifested, that he might destroy the works of the devil. [9]Whosoever is born of God doth not commit sin; for his seed remaineth in him: and he cannot sin, because he is born of God. [10]In this the children of God are manifest, and the children of the devil: whosoever doeth not righteousness is not of God, neither he that loveth not his brother. [11]For this is the message that ye heard from the beginning, that we should love one another.

God is Love

Chapter 4

BELOVED, LET US LOVE ONE ANOTHER: FOR LOVE IS of God; and every one that loveth is born of God, and knoweth God. [8]He that loveth not knoweth not God; for God is love. [9]In this was manifested the love of God toward us, because that God sent his only begotten Son into the world, that we might live through him. [10]Herein is love, not that we loved God, but that he loved us, and sent his Son to be the propitiation for our sins. [11]Beloved, if God so loved us, we ought also to love one another. [12]No man hath seen God at any time. If we love one another, God dwelleth in us, and his love is perfected in us.

[13]Hereby know we that we dwell in him, and he in us, because he hath given us of his Spirit. [14]And we have seen and do testify that the Father sent the Son to be the Saviour of the world. [15]Whosoever shall confess that Jesus is the Son of God, God dwelleth in him, and he in God. [16]And we have known and believed the love that God hath to us.

Chapter 4

THE FOUNTAIN OF LOVE *by Jean-Honoré Fragonard*

Chapter 4

God is love; and he that dwelleth in love dwelleth in God, and God in him. [17]Herein is our love made perfect, that we may have boldness in the day of judgment: because as he is, so are we in this world. [18]There is no fear in love; but perfect love casteth out fear: because fear hath torment. He that feareth is not made perfect in love.

[19]We love him, because he first loved us. [20]If a man say, "I love God," and hateth his brother, he is a liar: for he that loveth not his brother whom he hath seen, how can he love God whom he hath not seen? [21]And this commandment have we from him, that he who loveth God love his brother also.

THE GENERAL EPISTLE OF

JUDE

Doxology

NOW UNTO HIM THAT IS ABLE TO KEEP YOU from falling, and to present you faultless before the presence of his glory with exceeding joy, [25]to the only wise God our Saviour, be glory and majesty, dominion and power, both now and ever. Amen.

Chapter & Verses
FROM

THE REVELATION *OF* ST. JOHN THE DIVINE

JOHN'S VISION ON PATMOS • THE MESSAGE TO LAODICEA • THE THRONE IN HEAVEN • THE BOOK AND THE LAMB • THE FOUR HORSEMEN • THE GREAT MULTITUDE • WAR IN HEAVEN • THE HARVEST OF THE EARTH • THE SEVEN LAST PLAGUES • THE WOMAN ON THE BEAST • THE RIDER ON THE WHITE HORSE • THE LAST JUDGEMENT • THE NEW JERUSALEM • THE RIVER OF LIFE • ALPHA AND OMEGA

Detail of THE LAST JUDGMENT *by Beato Angelico*

John's Vision on Patmos

Chapter 1

JOHN TO THE SEVEN CHURCHES WHICH ARE IN ASIA: Grace be unto you, and peace, from him which is, and which was, and which is to come; and from the seven Spirits which are before his throne; [5]and from Jesus Christ, who is the faithful witness, and the first begotten of the dead, and the prince of the kings of the earth.

Unto him that loved us, and washed us from our sins in his own blood, [6]and hath made us kings and priests unto God and his Father; to him be glory and dominion for ever and ever. Amen.

[7]Behold, he cometh with clouds;
And every eye shall see him,
And they also which pierced him:
And all kindreds of the earth shall wail because of him.
Even so, Amen.

[8]"I am Alpha and Omega, the beginning and the ending," saith the Lord, "which is, and which was, and which is to come, the Almighty."

[9]I John, who also am your brother, and companion in tribulation, and in the kingdom and patience of Jesus Christ, was in the isle that is called Patmos, for the word of God, and for the testimony of Jesus Christ. [10]I was in the Spirit on the Lord's day, and heard behind me a great voice, as of a trumpet, [11]saying, "I am Alpha and Omega, the first and the last": and "What thou seest, write in a book, and send it unto the seven churches which are in Asia; unto Ephesus, and unto Smyrna, and unto Pergamos, and unto Thyatira, and unto Sardis, and unto Philadelphia, and unto Laodicea."

Detail from St John the Evangelist at Patmos *by Hans Memling*

Chapter 1

[12]And I turned to see the voice that spake with me. And being turned, I saw seven golden candlesticks; [13]and in the midst of the seven candlesticks one like unto the Son of man, clothed with a garment down to the foot, and girt about the paps with a golden girdle. [14]His head and his hairs were white like wool, as white as snow; and his eyes were as a flame of fire; [15]and his feet like unto fine brass, as if they burned in a furnace; and his voice as the sound of many waters. [16]And he had in his right hand seven stars: and out of his mouth went a sharp two-edged sword: and his countenance was as the sun shineth in his strength.

[17]And when I saw him, I fell at his feet as dead. And he laid his right hand upon me, saying unto me, "Fear not; I am the first and the last: [18]I am he that liveth, and was dead; and, behold, I am alive for evermore, Amen; and have the keys of hell and of death."

The Message to Laodicea

Chapter 3

"I KNOW THY WORKS, THAT THOU ART NEITHER cold nor hot: I would thou wert cold or hot. [16]So then because thou art lukewarm, and neither cold nor hot, I will spue thee out of my mouth. [17]Because thou sayest, 'I am rich, and increased with goods, and have need of nothing'; and knowest not that thou art wretched, and miserable, and poor, and blind, and naked: [18]I counsel thee to buy of me gold tried in the fire, that thou mayest be rich; and white raiment, that thou mayest be clothed, and that the shame of thy nakedness do not appear; and anoint thine eyes with eyesalve, that thou mayest see.

[19]"As many as I love, I rebuke and chasten: be zealous therefore, and repent. [20]Behold, I stand at the door, and knock: if any man hear my voice, and open the door, I will come in to him, and will sup with him, and he with me.

[21]"To him that overcometh will I grant to sit with me in my throne, even as I also overcame, and am set down with my Father in his throne. [22]He that hath an ear, let him hear what the Spirit saith unto the churches."

The Throne in Heaven

Chapter 4

AFTER THIS I LOOKED, AND, BEHOLD, A DOOR WAS opened in heaven: and the first voice which I heard was as it were of a trumpet talking with me; which said, "Come up hither, and I will shew thee things which must be hereafter." [2]And immediately I was in the spirit: and, behold, a throne was set in heaven, and one sat on the throne. [3]And he that sat was to look upon like a jasper and a sardine stone: and there was a rainbow round about the throne, in sight like unto an emerald. [4]And round about the throne were four and twenty seats: and upon the seats I saw four and twenty elders sitting, clothed in white raiment; and they had on their heads crowns of gold. [5]And out of the throne proceeded lightnings and thunderings and voices: and there

JOACHIM'S SACRIFICE *by Ambrogio Bondone Giotto*

Chapter 4

were seven lamps of fire burning before the throne, which are the seven Spirits of God.

[6]And before the throne there was a sea of glass like unto crystal: and in the midst of the throne, and round about the throne, were four beasts full of eyes before and behind. [7]And the first beast was like a lion, and the second beast like a calf, and the third beast had a face as a man, and the fourth beast was like a flying eagle. [8]And the four beasts had each of them six wings about him; and they were full of eyes within: and they rest not day and night, saying,

"Holy, holy, holy,
Lord God Almighty,
Which was, and is, and is to come."

[9]And when those beasts give glory and honour and thanks to him that sat on the throne, who liveth for ever and ever, [10]the four and twenty elders fall down before him that sat on the throne, and worship him that liveth for ever and ever, and cast their crowns before the throne, saying,

[11] "Thou art worthy, O Lord,
To receive glory and honour and power:
For thou hast created all things,
And for thy pleasure they are and were created."

The Book and the Lamb

Chapter 5

AND I SAW IN THE RIGHT HAND OF HIM THAT SAT on the throne a book written within and on the backside, sealed with seven seals. [2]And I saw a strong angel proclaiming with a loud voice, "Who is worthy to open the book, and to loose the seals thereof?" [3]And no man in heaven, nor in earth, neither under the earth, was able to open the book, neither to look thereon. [4]And I wept much, because no man was found worthy to open and to read the book, neither to look thereon. [5]And one of the elders saith unto me, "Weep not: behold, the Lion of the tribe of Juda the Root of David, hath prevailed to open the book, and to loose the seven seals thereof."

[6]And I beheld, and, lo, in the midst of the throne and of the four beasts, and in the midst of the elders, stood a Lamb as it had been slain, having seven horns and seven eyes, which are the seven Spirits of God sent forth into all the earth. [7]And he came and took the book out of the right hand of him that sat upon the throne. [8]And when he had taken the book, the four beasts and four and twenty elders fell down before the Lamb, having every one of them harps, and golden vials full of odours, which are the prayers of saints.

[9]And they sung a new song, saying,

"Thou art worthy to take the book,
And to open the seals thereof:
For thou wast slain,
And hast redeemed us to God by thy blood
Out of every kindred, and tongue, and people, and nation;
[10] And hast made us unto our God kings and priests:
And we shall reign on the earth."

[11]And I beheld, and I heard the voice of many angels round about the throne and the beasts and the elders: and the number of them was ten thousand times ten thousand, and thousands of thousands; [12]saying with a loud voice,

"Worthy is the Lamb that was slain
To receive power, and riches, and wisdom, and strength,
And honour, and glory, and blessing."

[13]And every creature which is in heaven, and on the earth, and under the earth, and such as are in the sea, and all that are in them, heard I saying,

"Blessing, and honour, and glory, and power,
Be unto him that sitteth upon the throne,
And unto the Lamb for ever and ever."

[14]And the four beasts said, "Amen." And the four and twenty elders fell down and worshipped him that liveth for ever and ever.

The Four Horsemen

Chapter 6

And I saw when the Lamb opened one of the seals, and I heard, as it were the noise of thunder, one of the four beasts saying, "Come and see." [2]And I saw, and behold a white horse: and he that sat on him had a bow; and a

The Four Horsemen of the Apocalypse *by Albrecht Dürer*

Chapter 6

crown was given unto him: and he went forth conquering, and to conquer.

[3]And when he had opened the second seal, I heard the second beast say, "Come and see." [4]And there went out another horse that was red: and power was given to him that sat thereon to take peace from the earth, and that they should kill one another: and there was given unto him a great sword.

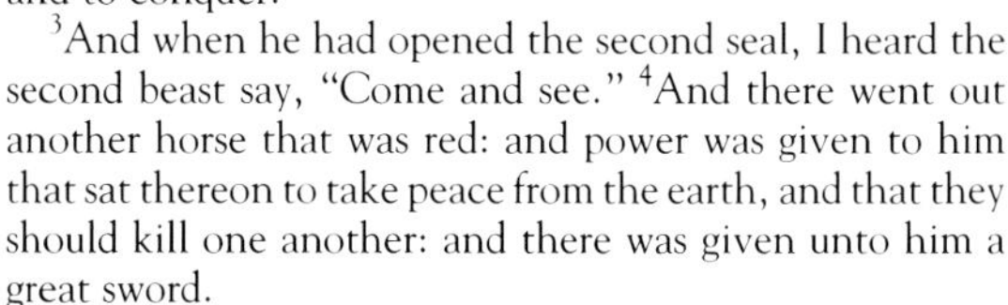

[5]And when he had opened the third seal, I heard the third beast say, "Come and see." And I beheld, and lo a black horse; and he that sat on him had a pair of balances in his hand. [6]And I heard a voice in the midst of the four beasts say, "A measure of wheat for a penny, and three measures of barley for a penny; and see thou hurt not the oil and the wine."

[7]And when he had opened the fourth seal, I heard the voice of the fourth beast say, "Come and see." [8]And I looked, and behold a pale horse: and his name that sat on him was Death, and Hell followed with him. And power was given unto them over the fourth part of the earth, to kill with sword, and with hunger, and with death, and with the beasts of the earth.

The Great Multitude

Chapter 7

AFTER THIS I BEHELD, AND, LO, A GREAT MULTItude, which no man could number, of all nations, and kindreds, and people, and tongues, stood before the throne, and before the Lamb, clothed with white robes, and palms in their hands; [10]and cried with a loud voice, saying,

> "Salvation to our God
> Which sitteth upon the throne,
> And unto the Lamb."

[11]And all the angels stood round about the throne, and about the elders and the four beasts, and fell before the throne on their faces, and worshipped God, [12]saying,

Chapter 7

"Amen: Blessing, and glory,
And wisdom, and thanksgiving, and honour,
And power, and might,
Be unto our God for ever and ever. Amen."

[13]And one of the elders answered, saying unto me, "What are these which are arrayed in white robes? And whence came they?"

[14]And I said unto him, "Sir, thou knowest."

And he said to me, "These are they which came out of great tribulation, and have washed their robes, and made them white in the blood of the Lamb. [15]Therefore are they before the throne of God, and serve him day and night in his temple: and he that sitteth on the throne shall dwell among them. [16]They shall hunger no more, neither thirst any more; neither shall the sun light on them, nor any heat. [17]For the Lamb which is in the midst of the throne shall feed them, and shall lead them unto living fountains of waters: and God shall wipe away all tears from their eyes."

War in Heaven

Chapter 12

AND THERE WAS WAR IN HEAVEN; MICHAEL AND his angels fought against the dragon; and the dragon fought and his angels, [8]and prevailed not; neither was their place found any more in heaven. [9]And the great dragon was cast out, that old serpent, called the Devil, and Satan, which deceiveth the whole world: he was cast out into the earth, and his angels were cast out with him.

[10]And I heard a loud voice saying in heaven, "Now is come salvation, and strength, and the kingdom of our God, and the power of his Christ: for the accuser of our brethren is cast down, which accused them before our God day and night. [11]And they overcame him by the blood of the Lamb, and by the word of their testimony; and they loved not their lives unto the death. [12]Therefore rejoice, ye heavens, and ye that dwell in them. Woe to the inhabiters

of the earth and of the sea! For the devil is come down unto you, having great wrath, because he knoweth that he hath but a short time."

Chapter 12

The Harvest of the Earth

AND I HEARD A VOICE FROM HEAVEN SAYING UNTO me, "Write, 'Blessed are the dead which die in the Lord from henceforth': Yea, saith the Spirit, that they may rest from their labours; and their works do follow them."

Chapter 13

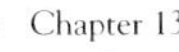

[14]And I looked, and behold a white cloud, and upon the cloud one sat like unto the Son of man, having on his head a golden crown, and in his hand a sharp sickle. [15]And another angel came out of the temple, crying with a loud voice to him that sat on the cloud, "Thrust in thy sickle, and reap: for the time is come for thee to reap; for the har-

ABUNDANCE AND THE FOUR ELEMENTS *by Jan Bruegel*

Chapter 13

vest of the earth is ripe." [16]And he that sat on the cloud thrust in his sickle on the earth; and the earth was reaped.

[17]And another angel came out of the temple which is in heaven, he also having a sharp sickle. [18]And another angel came out from the altar, which had power over fire; and cried with a loud cry to him that had the sharp sickle, saying, "Thrust in thy sharp sickle, and gather the clusters of the vine of the earth; for her grapes are fully ripe." [19]And the angel thrust in his sickle into the earth, and gathered the vine of the earth, and cast it into the great winepress of the wrath of God.

The Seven Last Plagues

Chapter 15

AND I SAW ANOTHER SIGN IN HEAVEN, GREAT AND marvellous, seven angels having the seven last plagues; for in them is filled up the wrath of God. [2]And I saw as it were a sea of glass mingled with fire: and them that had gotten the victory over the beast, and over his image, and over his mark, and over the number of his name, stand on the sea of glass, having the harps of God. [3]And they sing the song of Moses the servant of God, and the song of the Lamb, saying,

"Great and marvellous are thy works,
Lord God Almighty;
Just and true are thy ways,
Thou King of saints.
[4]Who shall not fear thee, O Lord,
And glorify thy name?
For thou only art holy:
For all nations shall come
And worship before thee;
For thy judgments are made manifest."

[5]And after that I looked, and, behold, the temple of the tabernacle of the testimony in heaven was opened: [6]and

the seven angels came out of the temple, having the seven plagues, clothed in pure and white linen, and having their breasts girded with golden girdles. [7]And one of the four beasts gave unto the seven angels seven golden vials full of the wrath of God, who liveth for ever and ever. [8]And the temple was filled with smoke from the glory of God, and from his power; and no man was able to enter into the temple, till the seven plagues of the seven angels were fulfilled.

Chapter 15

The Woman on the Beast

Chapter 17

AND THERE CAME ONE OF THE SEVEN ANGELS which had the seven vials, and talked with me, saying unto me, "Come hither: I will shew unto thee the judgment of the great whore that sitteth upon many waters: [2]with whom the kings of the earth have committed fornication, and the inhabitants of the earth have been made drunk with the wine of her fornication."

[3]So he carried me away in the spirit into the wilderness: and I saw a woman sit upon a scarlet coloured beast, full of names of blasphemy, having seven heads and ten horns. [4]And the woman was arrayed in purple and scarlet colour, and decked with gold and precious stones and pearls, having a golden cup in her hand full of abominations and filthiness of her fornication: [5]and upon her forehead was a name written, MYSTERY, BABYLON THE GREAT, THE MOTHER OF HARLOTS AND ABOMINATIONS OF THE EARTH. [6]And I saw the woman drunken with the blood of the saints, and with the blood of the martyrs of Jesus: and when I saw her, I wondered with great admiration.

[7]And the angel said unto me, "Wherefore didst thou marvel? I will tell thee the mystery of the woman, and of the beast that carrieth her, which hath the seven heads and ten horns. [8]The beast that thou sawest was, and is not; and shall ascend out of the bottomless pit, and go into perdition: and they that dwell on the earth shall wonder, whose

Chapter 17

names were not written in the book of life from the foundation of the world, when they behold the beast that was, and is not, and yet is."

The Rider on the White Horse

Chapter 19

AND I SAW HEAVEN OPENED, AND BEHOLD A WHITE horse; and he that sat upon him was called Faithful and True, and in righteousness he doth judge and make war. [12]His eyes were as a flame of fire, and on his head were many crowns; and he had a name written, that no man knew, but he himself. [13]And he was clothed with a vesture dipped in blood: and his name is called The Word of God. [14]And the armies which were in heaven followed him upon white horses, clothed in fine linen, white and clean. [15]And out of his mouth goeth a sharp sword, that with it he should smite the nations: and he shall rule them with a rod of iron: and he treadeth the winepress of the fierceness and wrath of Almighty God. [16]And he hath on his vesture and on his thigh a name written, KING OF KINGS, AND LORD OF LORDS.

[17]And I saw an angel standing in the sun; and he cried with a loud voice, saying to all the fowls that fly in the midst of heaven, "Come and gather yourselves together unto the supper of the great God; [18]that ye may eat the flesh of kings, and the flesh of captains, and the flesh of mighty men, and the flesh of horses, and of them that sit on them, and the flesh of all men, both free and bond, both small and great."

[19]And I saw the beast, and the kings of the earth, and their armies, gathered together to make war against him that sat on the horse, and against his army. [20]And the beast was taken, and with him the false prophet that wrought miracles before him, with which he deceived them that had received the mark of the beast, and them that worshipped his image. These both were cast alive into a lake of fire burning with brimstone. [21]And the remnant were slain

Chapter 19

with the sword of him that sat upon the horse, which sword proceeded out of his mouth: and all the fowls were filled with their flesh.

THE LAST JUDGMENT *by Stephan Lochner*

THE LAST JUDGMENT

Chapter 20

AND I SAW A GREAT WHITE THRONE, AND HIM that sat on it, from whose face the earth and the heaven fled away; and there was found no place for them. [12]And I saw the dead, small and great, stand before God; and the books were opened: and another book was opened, which is the book of life: and the dead were judged out of those things which were written in the books, according to their works. [13]And the sea gave up the dead which were in it; and death and hell delivered up the dead which were in them: and they were judged every man according to their works. [14]And death and hell were cast into the lake of fire. This is the second death. [15]And whosoever was not found written in the book of life was cast into the lake of fire.

The New Jerusalem

Chapter 21

AND I SAW A NEW HEAVEN AND A NEW EARTH: FOR the first heaven and the first earth were passed away; and there was no more sea. [2]And I John saw the holy city, new Jerusalem, coming down from God out of heaven, prepared as a bride adorned for her husband. [3]And I heard a great voice out of heaven saying, "Behold, the tabernacle of God is with men, and he will dwell with them, and they shall be his people, and God himself shall be with them, and be their God. [4]And God shall wipe away all tears from their eyes; and there shall be no more death, neither sorrow, nor crying, neither shall there be any more pain: for the former things are passed away."

[5]And he that sat upon the throne said, "Behold, I make all things new." And he said unto me, "Write: for these words are true and faithful."

[6]And he said unto me, "It is done. I am Alpha and Omega, the beginning and the end. I will give unto him that is athirst of the fountain of the water of life freely. [7]He that overcometh shall inherit all things; and I will be his God, and he shall be my son. [8]But the fearful, and unbelieving, and the abominable, and murderers, and whoremongers, and sorcerers, and idolaters, and all liars, shall have their part in the lake which burneth with fire and brimstone: which is the second death."

[9]And there came unto me one of the seven angels which had the seven vials full of the seven last plagues, and talked with me, saying, "Come hither, I will shew thee the bride, the Lamb's wife." [10]And he carried me away in the spirit to a great and high mountain, and shewed me that great city, the holy Jerusalem, descending out of heaven from God, [11]having the glory of God; and her light was like unto a stone most precious, even like a jasper stone, clear as crystal; [12]and had a wall great and high, and had twelve gates, and at the gates twelve angels, and names written thereon, which are the names of the twelve tribes of the children of Israel: [13]on the east three gates; on the north three gates; on the south three gates; and on the west three gates . . .

The Vision of St John the Evangelist *by Alonso Cano*

Chapter 21

[21]And the twelve gates were twelve pearls; every several gate was of one pearl: and the street of the city was pure gold, as it were transparent glass.

[22]And I saw no temple therein: for the Lord God Almighty and the Lamb are the temple of it. [23]And the city had no need of the sun, neither of the moon, to shine in it: for the glory of God did lighten it, and the Lamb is the light thereof. [24]And the nations of them which are saved shall walk in the light of it: and the kings of the earth do bring their glory and honour into it. [25]And the gates of it shall not be shut at all by day: for there shall be no night there.

The River of Life

Chapter 22

AND HE SHEWED ME A PURE RIVER OF WATER OF life, clear as crystal, proceeding out of the throne of God and of the Lamb. [2]In the midst of the street of it, and on either side of the river, was there the tree of life, which bare twelve manner of fruits, and yielded her fruit every month: and the leaves of the tree were for the healing of the nations. [3]And there shall be no more curse: but the throne of God and of the Lamb shall be in it; and his servants shall serve him: [4]and they shall see his face; and his name shall be in their foreheads. [5]And there shall be no night there; and they need no candle, neither light of the sun; for the Lord God giveth them light: and they shall reign for ever and ever.